WHO
RULES
YOUR MIND?

WHO
RULES
YOUR MIND?

Mark Armstrong

authorHOUSE®

AuthorHouse™ UK Ltd.
1663 Liberty Drive
Bloomington, IN 47403   USA
www.authorhouse.co.uk
Phone: 0800.197.4150

Published by AuthorHouse   05/08/2013

ISBN: 978-1-4817-9457-2 (sc)
ISBN: 978-1-4817-9466-4 (e)

CONTENTS

Introduction

Are you finding that life is ruling you, with some aspects of your life seeming uncertain, to say the least? If so, is this causing you stress? Do you desire for something to change in your life so that your world can become a better place? Are you experiencing a pattern of repetitive struggles or depression of some kind and find that you don't understand how to break free from this? Do you ask what the purpose of all of this is?

Many people answer these questions affirmatively, and I was one of them. My desire is for this book to set you on a path that will enable you to rule over your life with purpose rather than life throwing impossible-to-catch curved balls at you. This book is the result of my own personal journey in my search for finding purpose and peace in a troubled world where everyone seems to be on his own mission, leaving one feeling stranded. I found answers in finding my true self, but more than that, I found that I was not alone as my true self. I also found a part of me that seemed to try to protect me from further hurts and failures yet only made matters worse. I found that my mindset concerning God needed to change. I found that what I believe determines my world.

What is the purpose of this book? The best answer is that it will help you find your true authentic self and, just as importantly, help you become aware of a side of you that will sabotage almost everything that is good for you if it is allowed to rule.

The bottom line is that an awareness of your true magnificence needs to become a reality because up to now, you may have been on autopilot, living from data based on past experiences and using this same data to project into the future, which I doubt is worth getting excited about. I want to open your mind to a new dimension where you don't see yourself as the victim. I want to open your mind to a resource in you that is limitless and will allow you to grasp your own potential to change everything. This resource, this well of love that lies within you, has no end, just as the universe is endless. I want to lead you to this well, as it were, in order for you to discover your purpose in life and the limitless power that you have access to. As best I can, I will reveal the blockages that prevent you from experiencing more of your greatness which has in all probability for the most part eluded you up to now.

You may feel that this is a pipe dream I am talking about, but at the end of the day, the choice is yours. You may already be saying that this is no good and will be of little use, that nothing is going to change and you don't really deserve any better anyway. These voices cripple you. I want to raise an awareness in you that was never there before: an awareness of those voices and an awareness of your false self and how it operates so that you can recognise the folly of its ways. It is time for you to find your true self, which was made in the image of your Creator. It is time for you to become aware of your false self and the deception that occurs from this side of you, which will sabotage you in attempting to find your true self. You may say that you have tried this spiritual stuff, but I ask you to give me an opportunity to lead you to a place where you can see how fear rules you, how it cripples any chances of lasting positive change in your life. As you discover your true self, you will laugh in the face of difficulties as you grasp the greatness in who you are. Above all, you will find that love is all around you, that you were in fact pushing it away without realising what you were doing.

You may be feeling isolated and alone, with no one seeming interested in listening to your story or trying to understand. Maybe I can help simply because I do care. So who am I? I would describe myself as a normal guy, born in 1954 into what I would regard as a functional family unit for the most part. From my first marriage, I have a son in the United Kingdom, and he has grown up to be a wonderful man. I live in Pretoria, South Africa, with my dear wife and our two daughters, who are simply lovely and bring much joy to my life.

I know that I have found a source that flows through me, somehow changing everything, and my desire is for you to find something similar. I personally have experienced much despair and heartache at times, and I could not speak with any form of authority if I had not been in that place myself. The details of my experiences are not important. What is important is for you to experience an awakening of your true self within you, to help you find that power of love in you in order to change your life. I want to share what has been placed in me to help you in your quest to find the freedom and the abundance of life that is yours. It is yours because you are a glorious being made as part of this glorious universe. You are nothing less than magnificent, and I will mention this numerous times so bear with me, as this needs to become a reality for you. Your Creator sees you in the perfection that you were made. Yahweh, God, or whatever else you want to call the all-encompassing power of love that created you cheers you on to find your true authentic self. It has always been there but has become obscured by your life's experiences and your interpretation of them.

You are unique. There is no other like you. As such, the universe wants to play its music through you, the type of music that only you can play because there is simply no one else who can play the same glorious music as you.

This book started as a means for me to try to understand my own life scenarios, where there were times of lack causing untold stress in addition to family relationships which seemed to fly and then come tumbling down. I knew I was missing something. I went to church from when I was a small boy, with a perception that doing so would enable me to find life, only to be disappointed to find that it was a false sense of security.

My life has changed through the teacher I found in me, and I want you to find your own teacher, for at the end of the day, you need nothing from me or anyone else except to be pointed in the right direction. You simply need to be provided with the choices that only you can make so that you can be free to be your true self.

As long as you are ready to be helped, I know that I can help you change everything. The wonderful and strange thing is that the helper is in you and has always been there. My desire is for this book to be a tool in assisting you to get to a place of spiritual awareness of your true magnificence and the access you have to an energy source, a love source that eludes most of us.

The time has come for you to change everything through a renewed awareness of your divine nature which is your true self. It is time for everything to change in your life. It's time for the negative impact that life has had on you, because of not knowing your true self, to end. Not understanding who you are creates a limiting energy around you rather than a limitless energy.

I believe that reading this book will enable you, through an awareness of how you are made, to change your present mindset as well as those beliefs that hamper you from finding life the way it was meant for you.

Above all, I know that this book will help you break free from your misery and enter a place of fullness, a place where you can love yourself. We each have a side of us that is self-destructive in nature and for the most part creates havoc in one's life. We grow up believing that this is all that we are, unaware of the truth, which is that there is a part of us that is immortal, that is everlasting, that is love, that is our friend.

For the most part, we have a belief that circumstances must change in order for change to come to our lives, when the truth of the matter is that only we need to change in order for the circumstances to change.

In order for our lives to change, something needs to change in our minds in order to bring that change. This process starts with the knowledge that we need to be aware that there are two sides to each of us. These two sides influence our moment-by-moment thoughts and emotions, and there needs to be a constant awareness of which side is ruling at any given moment. To this end, it is important that you grasp the meaning of the following three definitions which I use throughout this book in an effort to simplify the process for you and allow you to grasp the awareness of these two sides of you.

Your true self

This is the real you, your true self, your true identity, created in the image of your Creator, who is Spirit. As a spirit being, you are love itself and everything that encompasses love, such as kindness, patience, compassion, and the power that comes with love. The spirit you is all good; it is grateful for everything and sees only beauty in all. It will radiate love just as its Creator is love. It can also be referred to as your divine nature, your inner consciousness. Your divine nature is righteous; there is no judgement, there is no shame, and there is no offence. It operates in the now and is able to expand into the future, not being threatened by the changes that go with this. Divine is a mindset that identifies only with love, limitlessness and abundance. Divine is a part of you, but life comes along and clouds the existence of your divine nature. Let's give this spirit side of you the name Divine.

Your false self

This side of you strives to form an exaggerated sense of self-importance and a feeling of superiority, always striving to be right. It thrives on judgement as a means to elevate itself. It is often referred to as ego. This is not a healthy ego required to function in a balanced state but rather a selfish mindset—that all-important 'I'—that will focus inward, with little concern for others. It is that part of you that is offended when not able to have its own way or when not treated the way it wants or expects to be treated. It is that part of you that tries to protect from further hurts and disappointments but in the process restricts all possibilities of finding a life that matters. It can also be referred to as your human nature.

This false side operates from past memories stored mainly within your subconscious mind, projecting these memories into the future, without the ability to operate in the present moment. It is that part of you that reacts without thinking of the consequences. It identifies with limitation, lack, fear and of being a victim and needs to protect itself. If you will, let's give this side of you the name Human.

Awareness

I want to introduce you to a third character, which we will call Sam. Sam is that awareness which makes you conscious of who is the thinker of your thoughts, at any given moment namely Divine or Human. This awareness then brings you to a place of choice. Sam in you is the beginning of the end of Human's controlling nature as you are then able to make the choice for Divine to rule through love, that has no conditions attached to it. With this mindset you activate the power of that love in you and your world changes.

PART 1:
STATUS QUO

Let's agree that change needs to occur in our lives in order for any form of change to manifest. How we go about this change is the crux of the matter. We read books which seem to help us for a day or two, and before we know it, we are in the same hole of despair and frustration, with life and all its demands seeming to consume us.

I want this book to be the spark that gives you hope, the spark that begins the mind shift that is required for your Divine to rule, changing your life, making it a wonderful place. With this renewed mindset what would previously have been regarded as obstacles will be mere stepping stones to greater things. Because of life's experiences in a world where Human rules for the most part, Divine as your true self has been hidden by your Human. The lack of awareness (Sam) of your Human and Divine which are both integral parts of you, has prevented you from being able to make that free will choice as to which is to rule at any given time.

Divine enables you to play your own unique music to a world that needs to hear your music. This may take the form of a smile to someone who is feeling desperate and alone. You will find that it's not what you can get out of life but rather what life can get out of you because of your greatness as a spirit being. That part of you that has been for the most part lying dormant needs to become alive through a renewed mindset. There is an unlimited source within you that may have been hidden by Human as your false self, and it's time for Human to step down as the ruler. Don't allow Human to condemn you at this point, the mistakes and regrets of the past are the past and divine will bring healing as you allow Divine to rule.

To answer the question of what life is about, I would answer as follows: It's about creating a life that matters, and a life that matters is when something far greater than your ego rules. A life that matters needs Divine as the thinker, that spirit being that you are as your true self.

CHAPTER 1

Who Rules?

As we grow up, we all experience situations and circumstances which cause us to believe that we are incomplete within ourselves. The most damage appears to occur from birth until about the age of ten. The opposite also applies in that if we are taught in our early years how wonderfully made we are and believe that, our world will be a much better place. Most of us have experienced situations where we have felt that we are not wonderful people, to say the least. This may have been caused by some form of abuse or a simple thoughtless act like being told by Mom or Dad to eat in the kitchen when visitors arrive for a meal, when you know that space could be made for you at the table. This lack of sensitivity to your feelings could find you questioning your worth. Altogether, life has a way of preventing us from feeling unique and wonderfully made, and we question our self-worth, losing sight of our likeness to our Creator and the power we have within us to change everything as our true selves (Divine).

We struggle through life trying to find happiness, health, and wealth—or something that might resemble those things—but we are searching for the wrong things. Without first finding our true selves, we will never find happiness, peace, or anything that is important to us.

Our purpose is to find and get to know our true self which remains hidden for the most part because of the effect that Human has had on our minds and the beliefs that go with this. Our true self as Divine is limitless, the magnitude of its power to change everything, and the resources it has in its connection to its Creator will bring you the joy and happiness that is meant to be a part of your everyday life.

This concept of our true selves requires a mind shift because it goes against everything we have taught ourselves or have been taught either directly or indirectly. Why does this elude us? Because something in us does not want us to find this part of us, and we don't even realise this. I don't fully understand why this is so, but I found this side of me that sabotages what is good for me, where I made decisions that were doomed for failure from the onset, where I pushed away those who could have made my life a better place. In becoming aware of this side of me which I refer to as Human, I knew that it needed to take a back seat if there was to be any change in my life.

I knew that I was being deceived in doubting as to whether I deserved the very best. I also knew that until this Divine side of me ruled in my mind, I would not be able to find life the way it is meant to be—where I ruled rather than letting life rule me. I may have thought I was in control, but I was out of control, and some form of grace seemed to be the only thing keeping me from self-destruction.

The extent of this self-destructive force in the form of Human in us varies from individual to individual, depending to what extent we have allowed life to feed Human as our false selves. This in turn has a direct impact on our self-worth. None of us are in the same place, as it were. This state of self-destruction will also vary depending on the extent to which we operate within our Human mindset. The more we can become aware of our true selves as Divine, the more love and compassion will flow through us, with less judgement and less fear. The energy vibrations needed to create and bring about the changes will begin to flow. The blockages which take the form of wrong beliefs will simply fall away because they have nothing to hang on to or with which to feed themselves.

It is never too late for you to grasp the truth of your magnificence and thereby change your life. In this awareness, Sam will enable you to start taking hold of the truth, and in this you will experience a change in your circumstances that you never thought possible. Something needs to change, and the change comes about through an awareness of your greatness as Divine, as the spirit being that you are, at the same time being aware of Human and the pitfalls associated with Human. Whoever rules your mind rules your heart and soul.

Human is that part of your mind that manipulates you into thinking it is Divine, and it knows that once you grasp the truth of who your true self is, it will be the beginning of the end of its rule. Human will make every effort to get you to put this book down or convince you that this is for others and does not relate to you—or that this process of getting to the bottom of things is taking too long. Human will sabotage your finding Divine and the awareness of this needs to be remembered. Don't underestimate Human; this would be a mistake.

In this awareness, Sam will enable you to have a fresh look at your thoughts and from which source they are emanating. Human's influence over our minds differs in each one of us with the influence coming from a place of fear. Don't feel guilty if you are fearful. Fear has a purpose, just as Human does, but fear or Human must not rule. Acknowledge the existence of fear and let it be a signal for you to give over to Divine. Don't fight fear, for when you fight anything, there cannot be a surrendering; there can only be a surrendering when there is an acceptance. In that acceptance you are choosing Divine; and in Divine there is a letting go, allowing a much greater energy which is love to remove the fear.

Where there is love, there is no fear. Divine has access to your Creator, to Yahweh, to God, to the I AM in you. In that part of you, there is only love and an all-encompassing knowing that you belong, that there is no end to you, that you are part of a universe which is there for you. When you start believing this, fear will leave you and I want to help you get to a place where you start believing this.

Please study the following three diagrams in an effort to understand the consequence of our choosing either Human or Divine to rule at any given moment. It is difficult to grasp how we are made, but most of us are comfortable saying that we are made up of three basic parts, namely body, mind, and spirit. I see Divine and soul as being that spirit side of us that is eternal and immortal. And when Human rather than Divine is allowed to feed our soul, the soul will not be in a place of peace. On the other hand, when we allow our spirit, which is all good, and love itself to feed our soul, our soul finds peace, and in this we find the abundance of life.

From the diagram below, you will notice that in Sam a choice has been made for Divine to rule in love for that moment. These thoughts have no judgement, thereby impacting your soul with a positive life-giving energy that in turn impacts your mind with thoughts from a place of love, eventually becoming a default thought process where trying to be love becomes less of a struggle.

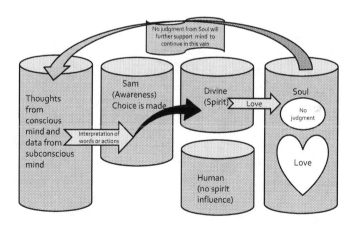

The next diagram reflects the consequence of a choice not to allow Divine to rule, even though there is an awareness that you are making a choice for Divine not to rule. In this scenario, there has been a free-will choice for Human to rule. This results in negative energy flowing to the soul. This is neither peace nor joy and in turn can further negatively impact your mind, whereby more of the same will manifest, namely more of Human, wherein Human becomes a default pattern even in the awareness of Sam. This mindset can be seen as a form of rebellion which sets you on a path of self destruction.

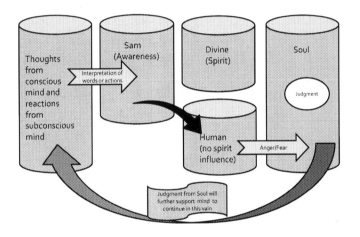

As shown in the following diagram the remaining scenario is when there has been no awareness, resulting in no Divine influence; Human then becomes our default mindset and has free reign. This also affects the soul negatively, which then can impact your mind/thoughts, reaffirming those wrong beliefs over and over.

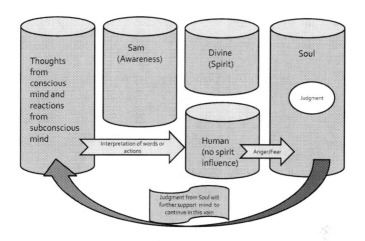

When thoughts bypass Sam, they go unchecked because there has been no awareness as to their origin, and without that awareness Divine has no influence, resulting in further judgement of yourself and others.

The condition of your soul influences how you are thinking and in turn impacts your world, causing either misery or joy. Divine as spirit has a direct relationship with its Creator, who is also Spirit, whereas Human operates only from an intellectual platform based on subconscious data stored from your interpretation of life's experiences, with no spirit influence. With a Human mindset, your interpretations of life's experiences will always be an illusion, as you will not be operating in the now moment but only basing your interpretations on past data which may well be skewed.

I also refer to soul as heart, as this is our inner core, the part of us that lives on after this life. Our hearts or souls can be found in a place of peace and joy or in fear, depending on which is the dominant ruler, Divine or Human. Remember, we are creators and will create either despair or joy.

What must change? Only your thoughts must change, and they change depending on the influence that Human or Divine is having on them which in turn comes about through Sam as that awareness of choice. Your thoughts can be your enemy or your ally. Up to now, the chances are that your thoughts and the energy you have created from them imprison you in a space that questions your worth, creating a blockage in your being able to receive the love which your Creator has for you as the Divine being that you are. The blockages come in the form of these wrong beliefs, for they create your world. However, the good news is that you can reverse the process by grasping the love that resides in you in the form of your spirit, namely Divine, and its connection to the universe, to God, to love, and to the life-changing energy that is there for you.

I suggest that you write down or copy the definitions of Human and Divine and keep referring to them until they are fixed in your mind. Human will generate negative energy because it thrives on judgement, while Divine will create positive energy because it is love.

For many years, I have been searching for the reasons that so many people, myself included, are not able to experience the fullness of life. I was raised in a good home with wonderful loving parents and did not experience any form of abuse in my growing-up years. Nevertheless, I have gone through life knowing that there is more. I knew that I was missing something; that the repetitions of life that I was experiencing were there because of something I was not seeing clearly.

Up to now, your life has possibly lacked abundance, which in essence is peace and joy. I believe that this book will help your mind get to a place where you experience the joy of love, knowing that you are loved and never alone. You may be feeling far removed from this place which is a result of you not being aware of what has been preventing you finding this place in your mind. This change comes about through a continual awareness of your Creator through Divine, allowing an energy source too big for us to understand to flow through you and to you. I know that you can experience a total shift in your mindset as you slowly, but surely choose Divine over Human to be in control.

Together we will create an awareness of your Human and Divine natures, and in this awareness, a choice can be made, allowing the false you, your human nature, to be exposed for the lie that it is when it stands up claiming to be your true identity.

This book is for you only. Don't read it and see someone else; see only yourself. Its purpose is for you to grasp what is happening in your life, to expose the traps that ensnare you, the destructive role that poor self-esteem may be having on your life, and the power of your subconscious beliefs.

This may not be an easy book to read. You may find yourself unable to concentrate on some of the material. You may become bored, angry, or even think about how much the book could help someone else. The reason for this is that the aspects of this book will confront your ego, your Human, so you need to be aware of this always. That part of your human nature (Human) can sabotage what is good for you in its ignorance of the truth. You will subconsciously hang on to your identity as you understand it.

Recognise the deceptions which have caused you to believe that you don't deserve any better. You may be poor, you may be rich, or you may have just enough, but that is not the point. The point is that you were made to experience a fulfilled life, a life that matters, a life that wants to love because it is love. I do believe that this book will assist you in rediscovering your true self as Divine, for when you were born, you were only Divine, and you have created your Human as a protective mechanism, thinking that you need protection, which in itself is an illusion. The process is to go back to your Divine, and you do this by becoming aware of the choice you can make: Divine over Human.

CHAPTER 2

False Self (Human)

Early in life, we learn to attach a kind of self-worth to the identity we create for ourselves. Somewhere between birth and adolescence, this process of self-discovery creates our perception of who we are, and an identity is formed. This identity is not set in stone and can change depending on what we believe about ourselves at a given time in our lives.

We commence a process of measuring ourselves against standards we create. Invariably we don't see ourselves as measuring up to certain standards, which begins a process of self-judgement. An abusive parent or a simple misinterpretation of a situation which made you feel that you were not wanted or not loved at a certain time can impact your self-worth and begin this process of self-judgement.

Poor self-worth is triggered from different life experiences. It may involve sexual or physical abuse or you having felt abandoned in some way in the past. For others, it may be an experience where punishment was given by a parent and the parent did not come back to reaffirm love. It could also be a situation when your brother or sister received a gift and you did not, making you feel less appreciated in some way. Thousands of these different scenarios play out during your life wherein you experienced a lack of love in some form and can cause you to question your worth.

The reference framework for Human is only from past memories. Human strengthens the wrong perceptions of how we see ourselves by continually trying to convince us of those wrong beliefs through the misinterpretation of situations because of our already skewed perceptions.

Human's position is always strengthened when the need for affection has been denied or insufficiently met. When parents are not at peace with each other or are caught up in their own struggles, there may have been insufficient affection and love given to you.

The false identity is often created when a child finds himself in a dysfunctional family. In most cases, one or more of the following situations occurred:

- Abuse of alcohol and/or other drugs
- Obsessive behaviour such as compulsive eating, working, cleaning, gambling, spending, dieting, exercising, and so on
- Battering of spouses and/or children
- Inappropriate sexual behaviour on the part of a parent towards a child, ranging from seductive behaviour to incest
- Constant arguing and tension in the home

- Extended periods of time during which parents refuse to talk to each other
- Extreme rigidity about money, religion, work, use of time, displays of affection, sex, television, housework, sports, politics, and so on

What all dysfunctional families have in common is the inability to address the problems by talking about them in a rational and meaningful way.

The children are not taught that they are wonderful spirit beings, and in essence Divine. Because of the lack of teaching and understanding, children will therefore automatically create their own ideas of their self-worth, resulting from their dysfunctional environments. Data will be stored in the subconscious minds of the children, causing them to portray themselves as not measuring up to certain standards. This data will be reactivated when they are confronted with situations where they feel they don't measure up, and they will go on the defensive, feeling as if they are the victim. This mindset has a downward spiral effect, resulting in further guilt and shame playing out their negative roles on their self-worth.

A dysfunctional home negatively affects your self-esteem, your self-worth, and ultimately the extent to which you love yourself; and the extent of your love for yourself determines the extent of your ability to love others.

Human will convince you that your present mindset, with all its never-ending thoughts emanating from past experiences, is who you really are. The noise generated from those never ending thoughts make it difficult for you to get to that quiet place where you can see your true self, where you are able to see clearly by being able to step back from the noisy place in your mind. Recognise the madness of Human and choose to distance yourself from this mindset, realising that there is another option in Divine. I don't want you to get discouraged, you will find Divine, this is a process and with a little help you will experience the joy of love which is what you are.

When you start understanding that you are not some kind of a freak but that there are millions of people experiencing what you are experiencing in different forms and ways, you will start feeling better about yourself. But this is not good enough, as you need to get to that place where you are your true self as Divine, that you are unique and wonderfully made. None of us on this planet is perfect in that we all have Human to deal with, but there must be no condemnation in this. It is not something we fight; it is rather something we recognise and accept, knowing that in Sam (awareness), we will experience the mind shift required to change everything.

Human operates solely in a time capsule, thereby causing almost every thought you think to be dependent on past and/or expected future data. On the other hand, Divine operates in the now and is not connected to time frames, only releasing positive energy based on love rather than past data. Teaching yourself to be aware of the now moment rather than relying on information gathered from the past is one of the main components behind the mind shift needed for Divine to rule.

Research indicates that our memories are also stored in the cells of our bodies in a form of energy which is linked to our brains. Memories are always in the form of an image, and these memories are then transferred to our brains in the form of that image. The book *The Healing Code*, by Alexander Loyd, PhD, and Ben Johnson, MD, states the following:

> All data, everything that happens to us, is encoded in the form of cellular memories. Some of them contain destructive, wrong beliefs that cause the body's stress response to be activated when it shouldn't, which turns off the immune system and causes literally every problem in our lives that we know of. The substance of these cellular memories is a destructive energy pattern in the body.

Human operates from a place in our subconscious minds where these memories can be recalled at any given moment. This in turn creates tension because of the negative emotions that can be generated from our mind pictures. We are unaware of these images in our subconscious minds, nevertheless, they are there and we react accordingly. This, then, is how Human operates from the past and never from an awareness of the now moment, where you become aware that you are not in the other person's shoes and this is good reason to simply listen without preconceived ideas that centre around judgment of others or yourself.

For example, if children experience rejection in their early years, these memories are stored in the subconscious mind. From this position, certain situations are often construed to have everything to do with rejection because of a reactivation of these negative memories in the subconscious mind, when in fact the present situation may have nothing to do with rejection. Even if it did, the emotion associated with rejection is often over the top. People get hurt, and when this happens, they try to find the reason for the madness of their reactions with their conscious minds. However, they soon realise that this borders on the ridiculous because there are no valid reasons to be found for the sudden reaction. Human relies on past data to resolve present challenges, only resulting in further pain of some kind. Unfortunately, the perceptions we have of ourselves are fed when we interpret thousands of situations as supporting those wrong beliefs. These wrong beliefs in yourself or about others, specifically those dear people that you are close to, can become so entrenched within your subconscious that I see them becoming, what I call strongholds, putting you on a destructive course that will cause you to alienate yourself from those that do care for you.

Awareness, or Sam, will help you to be sensitive to what is happening in these moment-by-moment situations. Sam provides you with a choice, a free-will choice to choose to proceed with your Human or your Divine. Your Divine as your true self sees your situations through a completely different mindset, where love and compassion is found with no judgement of yourself or others. If you find yourself not agreeing with me right now, recognise the possibility of your Human trying to justify your past reactions. It is a given that Human will be shouting from the sidelines as you consider choosing Divine's way, for this process strips Human of the control it has had up to now. Don't fight Human. Accept it, knowing that Human wants to protect you from a Divine mindset as it will see Divine as madness. Divine must rule as your true self and we will discuss later in more detail why Divine needs no protection.

Be aware not only of your own situation but also the situation that so many others find themselves in. Realise that others struggle within themselves as well. When someone reacts to you in some rather surprising way, it is their Human causing their buttons to be pushed as a form of defence, leaving you at the receiving end of an unexpected emotional outburst. Remember Sam, for Sam will enable you not to judge in these situations, instead allowing compassion to be present.

The way Human operates is to act without thinking of anything else but its position, which is a completely self-centred place. The consequence of reacting to subconscious memories and how this sabotages any form of intimacy needs to be recognised.

You may find that because of circumstances you are experiencing, fear grips you. Your thoughts run to places you fear. That victim mode kicks in, and you feel you must fight or run. Precondition your concious mind to stop, step back, and be aware of what is happening—be aware of Human—because once again, your subconscious data is at work, reminding you of previous situations where you felt the same vulnerability. That stepping back, that awareness of not simply reacting on autopilot is you choosing Sam.

It's the beginning of the end of Human and the destructive energy that goes with Human.

If you find yourself consumed with worry, be aware that you are feeling alone, when the truth is that you are not alone. Be aware that Human is in control at these times, and in order to get Divine in its rightful place, try different actions that will help you snap out of this place. As an example, concentrate on your breathing or a specific passage of writing that does something for you, allowing you to escape from the worry. The choice is yours. Understand that the worry stems from a mindset that needs to change

If someone calls you a name or labels you in some way, choose to connect with what the person is feeling rather than go on the defensive and seeing yourself as a victim. Here Divine rules, for trying to see the need in someone who is treating you unfairly can only be Divine. Recognise that this is love working and is the place we need to operate from.

Be honest with yourself and ask yourself how much love and success you deserve to experience. You may not be conscious of this, but you have set limits for yourself in experiencing love, wealth, health, and every other form of abundance. If at any time these limits start being exceeded by going beyond your preconceived level, you will subconsciously sabotage the situation, not allowing the further development of the positive change. Once again, this is Human at work because your subconscious mind has set these limits based on data you have stored from the way you have been brought up or because of the way you feel about yourself. You don't believe that you deserve anything above a certain threshold.

When you are operating from a mindset dominated by Human, you will find yourself subconsciously pushing those closest to you away rather than encouraging intimacy within the relationship. You do this by hurtful words spoken or being plain spiteful. Why do you do this? You do this because your needs are not being met because of your inability to love yourself. For example, suppose you say this to your partner: "You don't care; you are being inconsiderate." You may be making that judgement because you are feeling uncared for. Instead, say that you are feeling uncared for and express your need. You will find everything changing because this is Divine working. You will not be able to express your needs from a Human-dominated mindset, for Human sees needs as a form of weakness, when actually they come from a place of strength.

As your false self, Human wants to dominate because it does not take the form of love in any way; Divine, being love, will not dominate. Your brain is not a robot operating through instincts alone; it has the ability to always provide you with a free-will choice, a choice to step back with Sam. Sam then enables you to choose from where your thoughts will emanate, namely from a place of self-centredness (Human) or love (Divine). This does take practise in that you need to remember to be aware, but with time, it will become second nature, your Divine nature.

CHAPTER 3

True Self (Divine)

Divine as your true self is a spirit being made in the likeness of your Creator, and you need to start seeing yourself as the spirit being that you are. As you read the pages of this book, you will become aware of the person you are not. You will become aware of the illusion around your false identity that you believe in. You will become aware of Human working in you, making use of past data stored in your subconscious mind, which is unreliable at best, as this data has been created by your own judgements, your own interpretations of life's events from when you were a small child to this very moment. These interpretations were based on how you understood who you were at that particular time. Unless you saw yourself as the divine being that you are, with the resources in you to change the lives of people, including your own, through the unconditional love in you, then your interpretations of those life experiences will be skewed to the extent that some of the data or memories stored in your subconscious will border on the ridiculous and you won't even know it.

This awareness of who you are not as Human will facilitate the process of stepping back and noticing the role that Human is playing in your life. You will notice how your life is void of not seeing the perfection in your imperfection, of not seeing yourself in that wholeness, in that oneness, that you are with your Creator and everything and everyone around you. I do believe that you were born as this glorious being and you still are. You will start seeing how life has distorted this truth and the role Human has played in this process because of the absence of the knowledge of Human and Divine.

The better you feel about yourself, the more you will receive. Know that you will only allow to be given to you what you feel worthy of. You do not have to do anything to be a better person, for you already are that person. You were born perfect, and life found a way to push that perfection into a corner, as it were, because you did not understand your greatness. It is now a case of your grasping the truth in your true identity and understanding the role Human has played out in creating that false self. I know I am repeating myself, but these concepts need to take route through Sam.

I want you to start experiencing the fullness of life by experiencing the real you, the wonderful magnificent you, which up to now has eluded you owing to your not having Sam (awareness) continuously by your side, enabling you to sense what energy is emanating from you at any given time—energy created by Human or Divine, judgement or love, respectively.

The key is that your true identity is found in your spirit, in your divine nature. The power and the creativity we have as spirit beings to bring about the peace and joy we long for is within us; it is not found outside of us in the form of material things. I sincerely trust that as you read this book, your mind will be opened to the truth in who you are as Divine because this revelation will change the way you think, this will change the way you feel, and this will change what you believe—and what you believe you will create in your life.

Shri Mataji Nirmala Devi, who was born in India in 1923 and passed away on 23 February 2011, was an official guest in the former Soviet Union. She enabled over one hundred thousand people to experience self-realisation. She regularly spoke to audiences of ten to twenty thousand in the former Eastern bloc nations. She said the following, which is the truth I want you to get your head around, for these words of truth will open up the mind shift that you need to find the wonderful life of peace and joy that is yours:

> You cannot know the meaning of your life until you are connected to the power that created you.

> You are not this body, [and] you are not this mind; you are the spirit . . . This is the greatest truth.

> You have to know your spirit . . . for without knowing your spirit, you cannot know the truth.

Meditation is the only way you can grow. There is no other way out. Because when you meditate, you are in silence. You are in thoughtless awareness. Then the growth of awareness takes place.

The growth of Sam needs to take place. As Sam grows, there becomes an almost continual awareness of Divine. Divine (as your spirit) becomes a part of you that may have been hidden up to now for the most part. In the knowing of your Divine as spirit, there develops a knowing of your Creator, and in this knowing, love meets love.

Divine operates through love, thereby projecting mercy, patience, and kindness, whereas Human is far removed from any form of love. It is difficult for us to comprehend the magnificence of Divine. Within your renewed awareness of your true self as Divine, you will experience more of your Creator within you because spirit can only communicate with spirit. We need to experience a rebirth or a revitalisation of our Divine, and this occurs through Sam. The secret is not to resist Human, acknowledge Human's presence, but that is all. After all, Human is part of you. It's a case of managing Human with the assistance of Sam and Divine. Know that as Divine takes its rightful place as your true self, your thoughts, attitudes, and beliefs will change over time as you see things through a veil of unconditional love. You will see more beauty in all things, both people and nature. Let's look at some examples of how we need to recognise who we are not and in this choose Divine, who we are.

Suppose you were hurt in the past, when your partner was not loyal to you as far as relationships go. This caused hurt in the form of rejection. This created a need by Human to protect you from further hurt of this kind, and Human used the emotion of fear to activate a defence mechanism. This data or memory of rejection lies in your subconscious mind, and it is activated when any situation is interpreted to be associated with rejection. When this happens, your default reaction kicks in, which is to go on the defensive. This could take the form of words spoken by you that were uncalled for, resulting in hurting others and in turn resulting in further rejection—the very situation that you wanted to avoid. This is Human ruling, and an awareness of the results of operating from past experiences rather than from the now moment needs to be nurtured. This is a learning curve, but as you allow Sam to help you, you will become aware maybe only a second before you are about to react and avoid doing so.

Divine stands waiting to be introduced to the situation, a simple free-will choice on your side, activated through Sam. As soon as you make the choice not to focus on the past, where the 'I' is all important, but rather from a place of love, everything changes. Compassion and a willingness to try to put yourself in the other person's shoes is Divine at work. In this place, you will find the solutions, and the answers will come.

While Divine is the thinker of your thoughts, your mind will be dominated by a mindset based on the revelation of the real you, which is love, as your Creator is love. Where there is love, Human cannot rule because love will delete any form of fear which is the tool used by Human to rule.

What I am trying to explain is that we need to be aware of the workings of Human in that when we do speak without an awareness of where our thoughts are coming from, thoughts associated with a Human mindset will always be destructive in some form. They will certainly not be edifying in anyway. Only your needs are considered, not those of the other person.

Who you are not is Human, and therefore the manner in which Human has conditioned your subconscious mind with data through wrong beliefs needs to be exposed. In that exposure, there is a giving over or surrendering to Divine, allowing Divine to then take its rightful place as your true self. In this comes a renewed access to the Creator, to the universe, to Yahweh, to God, to love. I find it difficult to grasp who God is simply because of the enormity and power of this energy force. We all need to find ways to make God real to us, and because of our uniqueness, this will differ in each one of us. Personally, I see God as the universe itself in that I can't comprehend the magnitude and forces of the universe. To help me understand God, I also look at Jesus, also referred to as Yeshua, because in this man, I see God. I see a love that I know can only be Godly. This man hangs on a cross dying slowly in agony, having done no harm to anyone, only good, and can say, "Forgive them, for they don't know what they are doing" (Luke 23:34). I want this love in me because this love can only bring pleasure, happiness, and peace to all. I am sure you will agree.

As Divine, you have unlimited potential. You are blessed with abundant talents, gifts, beauty and love, way beyond what your thoughts can conceive. You have the power to change your way of thinking by allowing Divine to rule, which comes about through that awareness of the two sides of you. I know I keep repeating these things, but Human is stubborn and will try to block these truths, so repeating them will help you.

I want to provide you the means and the tools to enable you to take hold of the true spirit being that you are, becoming aware of the spirit you that may have lain dormant for most of your life. I want your spirit to become alive to your Creator, in the process becoming the creator of your own life, regardless of outside influences and experiences of the past.

It is critical for you to understand the importance of the Spirit of your Creator having an influence on Divine, which is that part of you made in the image of God. Therefore, it is also spirit. Your spirit needs to be connected to the Spirit of your Creator. As spirit beings, we need to become aware of the presence of our Creator in us, which is our source.

Can we agree that God is love, a source of creative energy that is universal? God is not male or female as a spirit being and is too big to be labelled in any way. I will refer to God as Creator, as love, as Yahweh, but know that these are mere words, and we need to move away from seeing God as this person trying to deal with each of our problems and wondering how he does this. This God is everywhere and in everything, which is too big for us to comprehend, much in the same way that we cannot comprehend that the universe has no end.

It is interesting that God is revealed as YHWH in the Old Testament. This Hebrew word translates as 'Lord'. YHWH comes from the Hebrew verb 'to be' and is the special name that God revealed to Moses at the burning bush. "And God said to Moses, 'I AM WHO I AM. Thus you shall say to the sons of Israel, 'I AM [YHWH] has sent me to you . . . This is My eternal name, and this is how I am to be recalled for all generations'" (Exodus 3:14-15). Therefore, YHWH declares God's absolute being—the source of everything, without beginning and without end. There are no vowels, so you can't pronounce the word. It's as though the writers of the Old Testament understood that God was unspeakable in a sense. In an effort to say the word, vowels were introduced and pronounced as YaHWeH and in the New Testament as Yeshua (Jesus).

Jesus shares the same attributes as YHWH and clearly claims to be YHWH. In John 8:56-59, Jesus presents himself as the 'I AM'. When challenged by some Jewish leaders regarding His claim of seeing Abraham (who lived some two thousand years earlier), Jesus replied, "Truly, truly, I say to you, before Abraham was born, I AM." Those Jewish leaders understood that Jesus was claiming to be YHWH. This was clearly established when they tried to stone Him to death for what they considered blasphemy under Jewish law.

What if YHWH (Yahweh) could be forever on your mind? What if you could see him everywhere you go? Wouldn't it be wonderful to be continually aware of this divine presence through a mind shift?

The awareness of your spirit, of Divine, is the key to unlocking and deleting the wrong beliefs that lie in your subconscious mind and feed your soul with limits to your identity such as "I am not good enough" or "I don't deserve any better." You may not even be aware that you are feeling these things. These beliefs lie hidden, sabotaging that connection with Yahweh.

Our subconscious minds are not all bad, for most of our bodily functions are managed from the subconscious. We can also have positive beliefs in our subconscious minds, enabling us to remain positive in sometimes difficult situations. The awareness of the energy coming from you is all that you need. If you are feeling compassion and mercy, then no words coming from your mouth will be interpreted to be other than kind and trying to help. On the other hand, if your energy is judgemental and wanting to blame others, what you say will be interpreted as such, even if you try to say it in a nice way. It's a case of what energy is emanating from you at any given moment.

The awareness of your spirit (Divine), namely a mindset of mercy and compassion, is you taking hold of your true identity. Remember that the mercy and compassion needs to also be directed at yourself because you are unable to show mercy and compassion for others if you do not show mercy and compassion on yourself. Your Creator is love, which is mercy and compassion, and that spirit-to-spirit connection between your Creator and your Divine only strengthens your knowing of your true self as Divine.

I want to introduce you to what may be a new concept, and that is the kingdom of heaven, which can also be referred to as the kingdom of God. The kingdom of God is a foundational aspect in the Abrahamic religions, namely Judaism, Christianity, and Islam, but what is it? It would be safe to describe the kingdom of heaven as the ways of the universe, of God. It's about a change of mind, of thoughts, of beliefs that will bring your soul to a place of peace. In reading the New Testament, one can confidently say that it was the purpose of Jesus (Yeshua) to spread the concept of being part of the kingdom of God, which is the mind shift required by you and me to grasp the reality of this energy source of love and of light that is part of us.

When Divine rules, you will find that you have a connection to a source that is the universe itself: your Creator, your Yahweh, your God. Here there is only passion for the weak and kindness, and in this place, you will be able to express that love which is not possible when Human rules. When Human rules, you know what is expected and you may try to show kindness, but you will not be able to express it in such a way that others can feel it.

When you were born, you were the perfection that your Creator made you to be before life tarnished that perfection. Maybe this is what Jesus, or whom I prefer to call Yeshua, meant when he said, "You need to be born again to see the kingdom of God" (John 3:3). You need to get back to that place of your birth maybe even before that, but I am the first to acknowledge that I know nothing about these things except that we started off as love itself. That is who you really are. Unless you can get back to that place where Divine ruled in you as a small child, you will not have lived. My dear friend, you are love, something so wonderful that your mind cannot grasp it, and that is the truth.

I tell you these things knowing that they are the truth, but I am also aware of my own pathetic Human and its self-centred interests. Don't allow condemnation from the past to make you feel that you are striving for the unreachable in Divine; this is Human trying not to lose control. We can all get it right to lose more of our egos and allow more of our spirits to rule. One step at a time. Your teacher is in you. Don't despair, for you are magnificent. I know that's the case, regardless of what you have done, regardless of how much hurt you may have caused others. I would be hard to beat when it comes to these things, yet I have found Divine. I know that I am loved by the universe, by Yahweh, a spirit being that I cannot understand except to know that we can all find the presence of this glorious all-powerful force of love. There will be no end to it. We make the choice to live inside or outside this presence of love, and my desire is for you to benefit from this book, to get closer to this love, to experience a life that matters, for you will bring healing of some kind to those that cross your path—but first yourself. You will touch lives, enabling them to be born again, to become more of what they were like as the glorious beings that they were at birth, before the experiences of life taught them otherwise.

To remove the blockages caused by Human that prevents Divine from ruling to the extent that your true self ought to is a process. The good news is that you don't need to fight Human. The blockages caused by Human will fall away as the awareness of Divine gets stronger, as that knowing of your true self becomes more real. Blockages need to be fed. They need something to hang on to, such as wrong beliefs, and as Divine rules, more and more of Human will start to starve. This side of you gets weaker, and those blockages fall away as they lose their grip. Your life will change in every way. You will have more than enough, and healing will come to your body. We will look more at the Kingdom of God in the next few chapters, because I do believe that the principles as explained in the scriptures around the Kingdom of God is where the answers lie in finding Divine.

My desire is that a determination will rise up in you, making you say, "Enough of the lies, enough of the negative beliefs, enough of the suffering. I shall go forward, and I shall rise up out of my thought patterns of the past and experience peace and joy as I become aware of my spirit (Divine) and the Spirit of my Creator operating together within me. In this, I will be able to show the compassion, the caring, and the love I so desire to have for others and myself."

CHAPTER 4

Awareness (Sam)

Remember to be aware at any given moment of where your thoughts are emanating from, i.e., Human or Divine. Be aware of your heart attitude. Have the words you've just spoken come from a place of mercy or judgement? Are the thoughts you've just had coming from a place where you are the victim or is it a place where there is no victim or victor? This awareness is the beginning of the end of Human's dominance and the beginning of a Divine consciousness where you experience a resource and power from within that is all love.

At some stage in your life, you have more than likely been aware of Divine, that spirit side of you, by experiencing something that you interpreted as being spiritual or supernatural. There was that something good that happened which you could not explain.

Be aware of not only your Divine and Human sides but also the two sides of your mind, namely the subconscious and conscious parts of your mind. The conscious mind is that part of your intellect that reasons and includes complex thinking, imagination, will, and memory; you are fully aware of its contents. The subconscious mind, on the other hand, is everything that happens in your mind that you are not aware of.

Various tests have revealed that your conscious mind is only responsible for 6 per cent of your behaviour and functioning, while your subconscious mind controls the remaining 94 per cent of your behaviour and functioning. For example, when you drive a vehicle that does not have an automatic gearbox, you do not think of pressing the clutch down every time you change gears. It becomes an automatic action. When you first started driving, it was another story, as you had to focus on the clutch while still looking at the gear lever and watching where you were going. You were using your conscious mind for all those activities, but later these actions became part of your subconscious mind.

The subconscious mind does not think or reason but rather accepts and stores all the information (such as how to drive a vehicle), including your life's experiences and the interpretation of those experiences. This information is never questioned by the subconscious. It stores it regardless of whether it is true or false. It accepts all information as real, accurate, and important, certainly not to be questioned. From information and data stored in your subconscious mind, you are constantly reacting to stimuli around you.

You will find that you may react in a certain way in a particular situation and not be consciously aware of why you behaved or responded in that way. This is Human operating from your subconscious, with no concern as to the feelings of others and the harm caused. Human does not think; it only reacts to preconditioned programming that lies within your subconscious mind and is based on your life experiences. This is the data that you have stored since you were born, and it is there to assist you, but where it goes pear-shaped is that the information stored concerning your identity is mostly wrong beliefs. If it were the truth based on your true self, which has no limits and is all good, then it would be beneficial in your daily interactions; unfortunately, 99 per cent of the information stored about your identity more than likely has its limitations. You are not even aware of this data, but it lies there and questions your worthiness and doubts your capabilities.

Divine uses love as its base because Divine is love itself. When Divine is the thinker, positive energy emenates from you, working with your concious mind, and in this the information becomes real time and valid, with no preconceived ideas or judgements. As you strive to be aware of the source from where your thoughts are emanating—i.e., Human or Divine—and in this awareness choose Divine to operate from that place of love, you will slowly but surely replace the data stored within your subconcious around your identity with the truth which is that you are love. Love that has no conditions attached, no judgment, only compassion, seeing the need rather than the uglyness caused by those needs.

There is always that free-will choice to make the effort to be aware of Human and or Divine and to choose from which source you will operate. It may seem strange not to choose Divine, but something in us is self-destructive. The expression 'You are your own worst enemy' comes to mind. Even though you are aware of Human operating in you through being selfish or simply spiteful, you will choose to remain in this place. Don't allow these moments to put you in a place of self-condemnation. They will happen as long as there is that awareness that you have chosen to remain with a Human mindset. You will get better at this; you will start making the right choices in Sam because you are good, even though you may find it difficult to believe in your goodness.

When there is no Sam, there will be no conscious choice of Human or Divine, and unfortunately, having no Sam will result in Human playing the domineering role.

You might find yourself overreacting in a given situation, and no matter how hard you try to reason why this happened, your conscious mind is unable to make sense of it. Here your subconscious mind has tried to protect you from a situation that it has interpreted as requiring some form of protection based on your past experiences in similar situations. You need to see clearly that this is not the real you, for it is not your true identity but rather Human trying to 'protect' you.

The awareness of Human and Divine will be that step that leads you to a renewed mind, where your true glorious self comes to the fore. In this place, you will understand that you don't need Human to protect you from what life throws at you, because as Divine, you need no protection. Understand that Human operates within its own strength, with no understanding of the limitations this brings. There is then no awareness of anything greater in you.

The energy from Human has only your own interests at heart and will only bring further discord within your daily interactions with others. On the other hand, Divine is love and will bring healing and comfort to those in need through you who may cross your path.

Divine is never a victim, is never offended, does not judge, and through love changes everything. This is not difficult; it simply requires a renewed mind that will come about through an awareness of who you are not. Understand that you have been caught up in this false identity, not grasping from a young age that as a spirit being, you have a divine nature made in the image of your Creator, and in this you have authority over your life. When operating from your human nature, you will question your identity and your self-worth, and life will have authority over you.

We choose love or fear, Human or Divine. Why do we choose fear rather than love? It is something we seem to do without knowing that we are doing it. We don't seem to be aware of the choice that we can make, and the reason is that we are unable to make that choice when we are unaware of our true selves and of the roles Human and Divine play out in our lives.

We fear something when we feel incapable of being able to deal adequately with the situation or we feel that we are not in control. We fail to see that we are creators who are more than able to create our own worlds through Sam and Divine. This does not mean that we will not be confronted with hardships, heartache, and despair. It is about how we react to the challenges of life because it is possible to experience peace even when all seems lost.

Having peace and happiness is a wonderful thing. It brings you to a place of your full potential. It helps to grasp your true magnificence and the source of love that is within you. To this end, Yeshua (Jesus) is recorded as explaining the following principle; this has helped me greatly in attaining this mind shift of not being a victim of your circumstances, but rather ruling over them.

History has it that Jesus called a young child playing nearby to stand next to him, and he said the following to people who were listening to his teachings: "I tell you the truth, unless you turn around and become like little children, you will never enter the kingdom of heaven" (Matthew 18:3).

Let's try to understand what this kingdom of God (or heaven, as it is often referred to in the scriptures) is. I can't see how it can be a physical place, for the following is recorded: "Now people were bringing little children to him for him to touch, but the disciples scolded those who brought them. But when Jesus saw this, he was indignant and said to them, 'Let the little children come to me and do not try to stop them, for the kingdom of God belongs to such as these. I tell you the truth, whoever does not receive the kingdom of God like a child will never enter it. After he took the children in his arms, he placed his hands on them and blessed them' (Mark 10:13-16)". "For the kingdom of God does not consist of food and drink, but righteousness, peace, and joy in the Holy Spirit" (Romans 14:17).

It would make sense to me that the kingdom of God is a place in our hearts. It is a mindset that impacts every part of our bodies and possibly every cell in a way that brings life—that is, no lasting sickness and no stress, only peace and joy. Let's agree that our present mindset needs to change, and it needs to change through an awareness of Divine and Human and the choice we have between these two mindsets.

Human rules when your mind consumes your every moment, and it does this mainly because of worry and fear. In this state of mind, you forget to remember Sam as the awareness which enables you to make the choice of choosing Divine—or you are in a place where you don't even want to make the choice. The kingdom of God is far from you when Human rules, for when Human rules, there is no peace and joy as in the kingdom of God.

Let's try to grasp what Jesus is trying to get across to us when comparing little children to the kingdom of God. Is he not trying to teach us to have a mindset of dependency on a greater power, a greater energy of love, on God? Is he not trying to say that only Human prevents us from entering this place of dependency, that dependency that children have on their mother and father, needing to feel their embraces as they provide the assurance that all will be well. Parents should support their child in every way, listening to them and caring for them. Is this not what we all seek? The truth is that your Creator is there to support, listen to, and care for you; and somehow you may think this God is far from you, when in fact this God is part of you, with a direct link to your Divine. Feeling loved and safe lies in a mind ruled by Divine, where Spirit talks to spirit.

Let's imagine the following scenario. You are living in your home as a small child with your mother and father, who provide you with a secure and safe environment. Mom and Dad are forever aware of your movements, safety, health, and happiness. Your father seems to have favour with so many people that you feel that you could ask him for anything and he would find it through one of his friends. His friends seem to be loyal and will do almost anything for him. At the end of the day, your mother and father tuck you in your bed and once again make sure that all your needs are met. You are able to talk to them if there is something troubling you, and they quickly put your mind to rest if there is anything worrying you. You feel their love for you as you slowly drift off to sleep. Your father always seems to be awake if you call him in the night because of a bad dream and the need for some reassurance. In the morning, you are awakened by Mom or Dad, and you know that you will be aware of their presence throughout the day. This is an ideal situation, I know, but let's imagine this scenario in our minds in an effort to grasp what Jesus is trying to get us to understand about the kingdom of God.

As a small child, you are aware of the love that encompasses you, of the reality that there is nothing to fear, that you are never alone. This mindset is what I believe Jesus is trying to get across to us. This mindset will change your life. It will dissolve that illusion of who you think you are,

41

namely a victim of circumstance, alone, someone who does not measure up to whatever and maybe does not deserve any better than the 'now' that you are experiencing. A small child in the scenario mentioned above will not feel as if she or he is a victim in any way. We only feel this way when Human rules in our minds. 'Fight your own battles' and 'Don't allow others to walk over you' are the pillars of Human's mindset. This destroys us because it causes pain and suffering and is far removed from the mindset that Jesus is referring to.

I remember going on holiday with my father, mother, and sister as a child. I would fall asleep in the car as we drove long distances to get to our destinations, the chatter of my mother and father dispersing into the background of my mind. I would have this feeling of joy because we were on holiday. I felt safe and not worried at all about getting lost on the way. Nor did I wonder whether my father had enough money to get us home. I felt only absolute peace. Life comes along and seems to change all that, yet Jesus says that you must become like this child, with a knowing that this higher consciousness, this God, is in the driver's seat. This God of love is in the driver's seat as long as you allow this through a mindset of Divine. Know that while Human rules, you cannot enter the kingdom of God, for Human is not found there.

The change in your present mindset from Human to Divine will require a choice, and you may well find that something in you resists this mind shift. This will be Human, your ego, that part of you that wants to justify your misery. Sadly, I have seen people choose to wallow in their misery, possibly because they fear leaving what they know, even if it is a miserable place.

What, then, is Jesus trying to teach us? He is saying that our thoughts need to focus around the concept of having a fatherly/motherly figure, as a small child has. Let's agree that we are talking about a normal functional family unit, with the child knowing that his parents love him. In this, there is no fear and no condemnation. A small child will have absolute trust in his parents, will be forgiving, will be grateful for what he is given, will know that he is not alone, will know that there are no conditions attached to the love of his parents. Because of the safety of the home environment, he will not have a victim mentality. This must be the kingdom of God, a place where we are at peace.

Can you see what this man Jesus was trying to get across to us? I cannot see Jesus telling us to obtain a mindset that is not obtainable. Those childlike qualities are within us in the form of Divine. It does require a decision to remember to be aware of Divine and for our thoughts to emanate from the place where our true identities are found.

Another Human quality that blocks us from acquiring Divine to rule is the way we may have been taught not to express feelings. A child expresses his or her feelings because life has not yet taught them otherwise. When a child has a need, you know about it, for the need can be expressed through crying. Once the need is known, it can then be taken care of. Then there is peace. As we grow up and experience life, we are taught that expressing a need is a form of weakness. After all, we must fight our own battles and look after ourselves because no one else will, and this is implanted in one's subconscious, where it lies and creates a default action for us not to want to express our needs.

Let your Creator know how you are feeling. In the simplicity of this, you will experience the miracles you long for. Once again, it is getting closer to the kingdom of God in you. You may well have entered into the kingdom, but you may be living like a hermit within that kingdom. Be aware of expanding your horizons and getting to know its wonder and beauty.

Being transparent and expressing your needs is something we are taught to approach with extreme caution. This is all utter nonsense; more than that, it is self-destructive. When your needs are not met, this impacts the needs of others, which are then not met, because if you are in a bad place, how can you be supportive in meeting the needs of others?

Be aware of Human, who will try to keep you in the place you are. You may wonder how your Creator can love you since you have done this or that. You may wonder how you can experience peace and joy, which is the kingdom of God, when you may have brought so much pain to so many people. Listen to me: this is Human at work. The truth is, we all need unconditional love, for we all have our Humans and none of us deserve anything good. Remember it's not about deserving anything it's about your position with your Creator. It's that mindset that says "yes I am loved by my Creator as a child is loved by his or her parent." There are no conditions attached to the love of your Creator. I know this may be difficult for your mind to get around, but your Divine knows this, although Human will simply not accept this, as this truth makes it difficult for Human to justify the misery that it so often creates.

The unconditional love is yours because your Creator made you and loves you regardless of what you may have done, just as parents love their children even though they mess up. Everything has been done in the spiritual world for you to experience that unconditional love, where there is no condemnation. Through Divine you will experience this don't allow Human to rob you of this life changing

If you are reading this book because you know that there is more to life than what you are experiencing, I know you will find the truth—that you are wonderfully made as a spirit being with a human body. As a spirit being made in the image of your Creator, you are perfect. I want you to experience this as a revelation for yourself, finding the abundance, peace, love, and joy you long for, ridding yourself of any idea that you deserve anything less.

My assumption is that on a scale of one to ten, with ten being at a place where you can love yourself because you believe that you are good, at least 80 per cent of us give ourselves a score of between three and six. The truth is you are a ten. As a spirit being, you are good, and my desire is for you to start believing that. Yes, Human is still a part of us, but Sam is there to ensure that awareness of love that surrounds you, that the whole universe is behind you, that as Divine you are a creator of good things, that you are able to bring comfort to others because of the truth in you.

When you were born, you were complete. All the talents, your creative abilities, and your perfection as a spirit being lay there in your mother's arms. In some cases, the little body may not be perfect, but it does not lessen the truth that you were born complete. Life came along and teach you otherwise. Your purpose is to rediscover your Divine as a small child. All you want lies within you; you need nothing from no one except for a renewed connection with your Creator where a renewed mindset enables your Divine to connect to love, to your Creator. In this rediscovery of your true self, you will find your talents surfacing, talents that will enable you to rediscover your true worth and a life that matters—a life that impacts others in a positive life-giving way.

The connection with Divine and your Creator makes you whole. Life is not a process of trying to become someone better than you are, for you were born perfect. Yes, imperfection has come in through Human, but you are Divine. You are magnificent, and nothing can take that away except Human. It's a case of Divine taking its rightful place in your heart. As you do this, you become that Divine being that you came into this world as. As long as Divine rules, you have that link with your Creator, which is easy when Sam is there, making sure that Human which is part of you, functions in its rightful place, which is not to rule.

Be fully aware that Human prevents you from making that connection with Divine and will want you to feel that you are a victim in some way. Human will always be on the defence, trying to protect you from further hurt, which disables your ability to find Divine. This need to protect yourself becomes centre stage and is a mindset only associated with your Human.

A change in your own beliefs needs to take place; otherwise, nothing will change. I want to encourage you to see change as a positive thing, not something that will bring further disappointment and hardship because this is what Human says. Our purpose is not to become more of something but to be what we are and to remain as such, to allow the manufacturer to restore us to our original specifications, if you will.

The fact that you were just one of five million sperm heading towards an egg and you won that race proclaims loud and clear that from the very beginning of your life, you were a miracle, so don't allow life's experiences to cause you to believe that you won't continue to experience miracles.

When we experience great loss, we do this in one of two ways. Either we experience a peace which occurs as we surrender to the situation, experiencing a deeper relationship with our Creator, or we see ourselves as the victim and resist by hitting back in any way possible. These thoughts create anger, resentment, and self-pity. It's either Human or Divine; the choice is yours.

Without an awareness of these two sides of you, namely Divine and Human, your life becomes misearable because Human will dominate your mind at all times if there is no awareness of Divine. Your Human is your own worst enemy. It tries to protect you but in the process imprisons you within walls of fear, bringing only loneliness and despair. We look at these walls in the next chapter, as there needs to be an awareness of the role Human plays in fear.

There is so much of the unseen world that we don't understand, but for now rest in the knowledge that a renewed awareness of your divine nature, of your Divine, and the power you have as a spirit being will change everything if that is your desire.

Be aware of the reasoning behind a Human mindset and the absence of a Divine mindset in any given situation, namely from a place of fear or love. Because love is transparent, Human will be shouting from the sidelines that you are opening yourself up to more guilt and shame and whatever other nonsense it can muster up at the moment. It is time to shut your Human up in the knowledge that you are love, and in love no protection is needed. Remember that as Divine you are operating from within the Kingdom of God, it is a safe place.

Remember that you don't need your walls created by Human when you are operating with a renewed mindset where love/Divine rules. This is a process, but with practise there is a mind shift, an entering into the kingdom of God. Human may be saying to you now as you read these words that this is not going to work, that you will fail and experience more disappointment and hurt. Recognise the trap and ongoing chatter of your mind being ruled by Human. You know what choice to make, and you have the power to make that choice.

Human will always want to judge; be aware of this. Stop judging yourself and those closest to you. Complete acceptance of yourself and others is needed. You need to see not only yourself but others in the perfection that they were made, and that their lives may have caused them not to believe in their greatness. There must be no victims, no accuser and no accused; this transforms relationships. Judgment comes from a place of weakness, although it masks itself as coming from a place of strength. Judgment does not come from a good place, so treat it with the contempt that it deserves.

When you are with someone you know will not judge you, do you not enjoy that person's company? The same goes for you: stop judging yourself and enjoy your own company. Love yourself and you will not judge yourself. Love those around you and you will not judge them. You are love and you were born love, so it's a case of getting back to that place, exposing Human and becoming aware of the breaking down effect that Human has had on you and the role you may have played in breaking others down. I think you will agree enough of the madness. It's a process of getting back to your true self, so don't get despondent when the old patterns hang on. You can do it. Remember that you are not alone in this quest to live out your magnificence as Divine.

The point is to be aware of any kind of judgement and know that it can only bring about a negative energy that will change nothing but only bring the repetitive negative scenarios around once again. Judgment separates us from Divine so please be aware of any judgment in you. Blame is a form of judgement so stop blaming yourself or anyone else for any scenario or situation in your life.

Human judges you based on your stored data in your subconscious mind, relating to your actions and reactions to life's scenarios. This data, for the most part, can make you feel wrong, and this makes you judge others to try to make yourself feel more right. If Human can't get this right, then it judges you for not judging others, and the madness of judgement therefore becomes all-consuming. Human always wants to be right; it will not say it was wrong. Even when you know you are wrong, Human will do its best to justify being right. Be aware of simply being transparent, which is a characteristic of Divine. Don't hide your mistakes, for this is Human at work. We all make mistakes, and those who want to judge us for those mistakes are in a sad place themselves. Also remember that Human is concerned about what others think of it, while Divine does not focus on this but rather on reaching out with love to the other person.

Human has its role when it comes to your completeness, but as your identity, Human is an illusion. The key is to surrender the control that Human holds over you, and you need to recognise how Human exercises this control in order to be in a position to choose to release this control.

CHAPTER 5

Walls of Fear

ecause of our uniqueness, the extent of the influence of the particular walls referred to in this chapter differ from person to person but still restrict us from being our true selves in Divine. We perfect many walls of protection over the years, but the five listed seem to do the most harm in blocking us from finding our true selves.

Fear is the opposite of love, and as long as you have a measure of fear in you, you will default to your Human mindset as a form of protection, for here you feel you are in control, which is the ultimate goal of Human. The strategy of Human is to create what we can call *walls for protection*. These walls are beliefs formed within your subconscious mind from life experiences, and once again, you don't realise that they are there until you find yourself reacting to words spoken, saying words that surprise even yourself. The spoken word or even the lack thereof will be perceived as a similar past situation that has caused you hurt, and you will go into a fight or victim mode to protect yourself from further hurt. The reality is that all these walls do is imprison you, blocking off any influence of Divine.

Let's look at some of the blockages that prevent us from establishing a mindset of Divine. These walls of protection need to be recognised for the destructive role they play out in your life. In an effort to expose these mindsets that prevent Divine from ruling, the following five walls have been identified:

Wall #1	Fear of being wrong
Wall #2	Fear of being a victim
Wall #3	Fear of not having enough
Wall #4	Fear of disappointment
Wall #5	Fear of not being liked

Wall #1: Fear of being wrong

Human always wants to be right so that the negative emotion of being wrong does not need to be experienced. Being wrong is not cause for a negative emotion with a Divine mindset, for you simply know that you have made a mistake, and there is no reason to feel guilty about this. Conversely, with a Human mindset, this can be seen as a weakness of some kind, needing to be defended. The reason can be that to be wrong further questions your identity, which in the absence of knowing your true self creates a victim mentality where you have to make sure that you convince yourself and others that you are always right.

As previously mentioned, your true self does not see making a mistake and being wrong as an issue. If there is a need to apologise, that is fine too. Recognise the need within you to be right, know that its source is Human, and understand that this is not the real you. Make a choice not to see being wrong as an issue of any kind.

When your view point is challenged and it causes irritation and anger, recognise that Human wants to be superior in any given situation and is offended when it feels that its position is being jeopardised in any way. If you make a statement and someone disagrees, how do you feel? What is the emotion that wells up from within? If it is offence, recognise Human operating. Remember that you are Divine; you do not have to prove anything to anyone. You are love, you are power, and a sound mind is yours. Sam is there to help you see what you are doing and help you choose Divine.

Human will justify criticism because this puts it in a stronger position of always being right, although if criticism comes your way, it is met with anger, as this is seen as weakening your position. Any form of criticism is destructive, and no good can come from it, so be aware when you try to justify this and realise the madness of it all.

Dr Joe Rubino said the following: "We will sacrifice our health, relationships, love, peace, possibilities and happiness just to be right. Give up your right to be right and your self-esteem will flourish."

Wall # 2: Fear of being a victim

Human takes everything personally because in Human's world it is all about you. This wall focuses on you as always being the victim, and therefore, for most of the time, you are on the offensive. You will find that there is an immediate impulse to go on the offensive if just asked a simple question if this is identified by Human as criticism, which in all probability it is not. You can be offended because you create conditions of how you are to be treated, and when these standards are not met, offence comes in.

Because of the victim mentality of Human, Human feels anger when you are wronged, offended when you do not get your way, and hurt when your opinion is not given the attention you feel it deserves. This defence mechanism is activated through anger, which will push people away from you. Reacting in anger to your partner when there is no clear reason for it is destructive. The person who is supposed to be your greatest ally would appear to be your worst enemy. Intimacy is lost, and it takes a long time to repair the damage this does to your partner. Remember, Human tries to convince you that nobody cares and that you have to fight your own battles. This is one of the lies that Human uses which causes such misery, and a feeling of hopelessness can come over you. Be aware of this and recognise the lie that it is.

Wall #3: Fear of not having enough

You may have this urge to store things that you have not used for years. It could be clothes, shoes, furniture, utensils, or home supplies. There is this feeling of never having enough money, attention, time, love, appreciation for your efforts, or anything else you can think of. It stems from an insecurity of who you are. Hiding behind material belongings does two things for you: it brings a measure of safety to you and makes you feel that you are of some worth. Human will do its best to convince you that you need outside things to make you feel whole and to identify with. If someone dares take or damage any of your possessions, you may have an uncalled for and embarrassing reaction. The reason is that you see these material things as part of you, so you feel that you are being damaged in some way if someone does not look after your possessions.

You need to be honest with yourself by asking yourself two things: If you lost everything, would you feel inferior? Would you feel superior to others if you had wealth? The point is, do material things have any influence on your identity. People facing death often realise that material things had nothing to do with who they were, and they see how meaningless these things are. Let us see the folly behind simply wanting more material things. As you find your true self in Divine, material things will follow, and although appreciated, they will lose their importance.

Wall #4: Fear of disappointment

In order to avoid disappointment, your thought patterns will not be positive. You will find the most ridiculous things to complain about, even when faced with something that you know you should be thankful for. By operating in this mindset, you avoid getting excited about anything, even when there is reason to do so. This screen cannot operate in a mindset of gratitude, so gratitude is something you will find difficult to show. By being grateful for something, you are acknowledging the joy that it gives you, and then Human reminds you that to avoid the disappointment of losing, it would rather stay as neutral as possible about any good thing that comes your way. A further reason for not showing gratitude is that you can open a door to intimacy to those you thank, and Human does not encourage intimacy, for this can bring further disappointments—and so the madness continues. The other component of not showing gratitude for fear of disappointment is that Human reminds you that you don't deserve this goodness in whatever form it may come in, so don't embrace it because then you may need to justify being happy, and Human does not want to find itself in that position.

Also be aware that somehow you might justify disappointment as a means to your own end, which is to convince yourself that this life won't get any better. When you think this way, there is less risk for disappointment. If someone asks how you are, Human will influence your mind to search for a negative response, as it does not want to get to a place where it has to acknowledge that not all is so bad—or maybe things are even great. Recognise this wall that you have built and make the choice to break it down by showing gratitude for everything.

Wall #5: Fear of not being liked

This defence mechanism is activated when in the company of people which may make you feel intimidated. With this screen, you play different roles for different situations hoping to be liked. This can become so important that you will not be able to relax in the company of others because of the stress that role playing can have, as it isn't easy to be someone that you are not. In the absence of not knowing who you are as a spirit being, there is little you can do to overcome the role playing.

Be alert to any satisfaction derived from imparting bad news about others. When doing this, it gives you a measure of satisfaction because it makes you feel important, as people pay attention to bad news, and therefore there is a better chance of being liked. You may even find yourself being dishonest in your efforts to dramatise the situation. Once again, be aware of this wall and challenge its existence by not condoning your actions.

You may recognise some of the five walls above in your life, and this must not bring condemnation. It must simply bring an awareness of how Human operates in your life because in this you will make the choice to stop the madness, as that choice remains yours.

I realise that talk is easy but be encouraged, for the awareness of what is happening will enable you to allow Divine to take its rightful place as your true self. Remember that you are not doing this alone; Sam is there to remind you of the choices you have. Remember to be childlike in trusting Divine, that spirit you who has a direct link to the universe, to Yahweh, to God, to Yeshua (or whatever works for you) when it comes to a higher energy of love that is all-encompassing and part of you. That dependency is important in that it shuts off Human and allows Divine to open a world that is dependent on you rather than your being dependent on the world. The world needs you. It cries out for your participation, which may be a smile to someone walking past you who feels forgotten and alone. Be aware of Human reminding you right now of when you have smiled at someone or befriended someone and felt that it was thrown back at you. It doesn't matter. As Divine, you will continue to show love when love or kindness is not returned because that is the real you. That is unconditional love, and in that is abundance because you are doing something from your heart, something you enjoy doing. I urge you to be aware of the lies coming from Human.

This is the question that needs to be answered: what do you want? If you want your life to change and experience the peace and joy that is yours, you will take hold of this, but if you don't really want this, you will simply continue with more of Human. You would not have got to this stage of the book if you were not serious about changing your life, so I encourage you to push forward and not get discouraged, for the breakthroughs you desire will manifest.

Your spirit is love, and it will see the beauty rather than the ugliness. It will be prepared to show mercy because of the awareness of how these screens influence the behaviour of all of us.

CHAPTER 6

Relationships

Life can hurt us in various ways mainly because we allow it, but nevertheless it hurts. These experiences have a way of distancing us from our true identities in that we may question our worth. We perfect the masks and roles that we create to 'protect' ourselves and to make us feel better about ourselves.

Over the years, Human creates a false identity in that our true self has remained hidden. Divine will bring you to a place that results in a complete mind shift around your identity. The foundations of Human need to be uprooted: foundations based on having to *look after yourself* because nobody else will and foundations based on the need to have *done good things* in order to feel good about yourself.

Human creates an illusion in forming an identity of who you are in your subconscious mind. As you read this, you don't even know what wrong beliefs lie there dormant, waiting to surface when activated by words and actions of others or feelings of disappointment when those close to you let you down in some way. Those wrong beliefs around your identity will surface whenever they think they can be reaffirmed by particular words or actions. Be aware of this pattern. Human needs to reaffirm those wrong beliefs repeatedly in an effort to strengthen that false identity. You will notice that this process revolves around judgement of others and yourself. Human will make you feel that you have to strive to accomplish love, work day and night to make ends meet, and feel guilty if you are having a few good moments doing something you want to do. Experiencing joy and happiness seems almost impossible as something in you seems to find reasons to be miserable rather than reasons to be happy, when in fact you know there is much to be grateful for.

Recognise how Human is operating and make the choice to do those things that make you passionate because of the shear enjoyment of doing them. In this place, Divine rules, and you become the real you, the you that can then bring joy to others because of the joy in you.

When you feel offended, Human is ruling because offense occurs when you are not in that place of knowing your magnificence in your true identity as Divine. Be aware that this is a sure sign that wrong beliefs in who you are lie in your subconscious mind are being awakened. Offence comes in when you interpret your wrong beliefs as being supported. For example, if you have a wrong belief of not being good enough in some way and you experience a situation in which you feel that you are not being shown sufficient respect, you are immediately offended. You will be ready to respond accordingly as you Human which now rules is feeling victimised, which will only bring more of the same because of your attitude and the negative energy that come with that. You are offended because your wrong belief, which is your own interpretation of events, is being supported, and this may or may not be a true reflection of the situation. If it is a true reflection, correct the situation without anger or spitefulness. You cannot receive something that you don't feel worthy of receiving, so no matter how much effort someone may put into showing you the respect and love which is yours to receive, you simply are not in a position to receive this.

So what happens when we get offended? Someone's opinion pushes our ever-sensitive buttons, and we react with a mixture of anger, frustration, and hurt. We don't care who we are hurting because we are consumed at that moment by our false self, which now has found some food to justify its misery. Depending on our nature, we either explode or isolate ourselves from the world around us by going into some form of hibernation or we go into the silent mode; either way, we now enter phase two, where we do our best to hurt those who have offended us. The game here is to be nasty and unkind through word or deed in an effort to get a negative response from the offender so that we actually have a more valid reason to be so miserable.

Why do we react in this negative way? Human has the upper hand; Sam is nowhere to be found. Wrong beliefs need to be fed in order to be justified.

Why do we have this need to justify our misery? Our poor self-worth needs to be justified.

How do we rid ourselves of the poor self-worth? Through Sam, we are able to make the choice of Human or Divine. In this, we make the choice to believe the truth or wallow in our wrong beliefs and all the negative thoughts that go with this.

Why do we not all make the choice to believe in our true selves, our true identities, as Divine?

Divine requires a surrendering to your Human self-centred mindset thereby allowing Divine with a mindset of childlikeness towards your Creator, with hope, trust and a knowing that all will be good to take its place. Not all people are prepared to do this because this can be a strange place, and Human will fear moving away from that known place even when it is a miserable place. Grasp the madness of this, for this cannot be life.

We all suffer from misinterpretations of situations from time to time. If you find that you are offended easily and take any form of criticism as an attack on your identity, Human will be happy with this response because it reaffirms your beliefs, wrong as they may be. The more certain you are of your misguided interpretations, the more control Human has over you, which can develop into a state of paranoia. Become aware of what is happening with any form of offence and do your best to react differently, acknowledging that there is that very real possibility that you may be being overly sensitive.

Your illusion of who you think you are affects your relationships with other people, especially those closest to you. Human fears intimacy, and getting too close and personal is an uncomfortable place because it makes one feel vulnerable. Human thrives on separation and feeds on alienation. Be aware of this need to avoid intimacy and how you will even unknowingly sabotage it.

We all try to find some form of justification for our misery. Whether it be the demons as depicted in *The Screwtape Letters* by S. C. Lewis, which do their best to manipulate our lives and keep us from Divine, or whether it be those subconscious wrong beliefs, it comes back to the fact that we are looking to feed those wrong beliefs so that we can feel better by being able to justify our misery. We feed those lies that tell us that we are no good, that we cannot experience life and the fullness of it because of who we are. The truth that we are sons and daughters of a Creator who is love, continues to elude us because of how we feel about who we are and that we may not deserve any better. The truth is you are the best, you are love and the very best is all that is good enough for you.

Close meaningful relationships with those closest to us are key in creating a life that matters, and when we struggle in this area, life becomes miserable. There are reasons that we don't reach the full potential of our relationships with our partners, friends, and children, and we need to understand that we have the power to change those relationships through the energy that flows from us; that energy must come from a place of love. Through Divine, you can do this. Mercy and no judgement is yours through a choice. The role of Human in your life needs to be exposed, for there is no other way. Human wants revenge. It wants those who have hurt you to be hurt in return. See how destructive this is for yourself and stop this. Realise that you are seeing yourself as the victim, which is your Human mindset something to be avoided as you focus on Divine.

How often have you looked at the relationship with your spouse and thought, *If only he or she could change, then I would be happier*? Welcome to the blame game, the art of avoiding responsibility when we find ourselves not having control over a situation and feeling victimised. We have this need to control, and this is only Human operating, especially when you believe that little is your own fault. You feel powerless to initiate the changes you want and thereby are freed from the responsibility of improving the situation. Through Sam, Divine will show these things to you. Through a renewed awareness of the unconditional love within you, of Divine, you will break the cycle that keeps playing itself over and over with your partner or those closest to you. If in the event of recurrences of these conflicts, be prepared to side step and rather be a spectator, thereby not allowing the emotional surge that would normally set you up for another round of conflict. By stepping back and allowing yourself to be a spectator rather than an active player, you refrain from acting as a catalyst in escalating the ongoing predictable conflicts. The anger, hurt, or fear that once caused these conflicts will dissipate as you let go, allowing Divine to take over. I know it is easy to talk, but this will get easier with practise.

Human says not to say anything because it is just going to cause more friction and unhappiness. So you keep quiet, not allowing emotions to be seen or heard. Then there comes that time when it all boils over and you find yourself saying things that hurt your partner more than ever. You say things that you truly mean at the time, no matter how void of common sense they may be.

What has really transpired here? The first thing is that Divine has been absent in this process. Divine would express the frustrations caused from the onset, not allowing a build-up of emotions. Because Divine will always operate in love and transparency, expressing your feelings may well hurt your partner at the time, but in the end, your partner and you are better off. There has been transparency, and even in the frustrations, maybe caused by your own imperfections, peace comes through because of the transparency shown.

When you choose to be quiet, you are keeping those walls of protection up by not saying anything because of the fear of hurting your partner or the fear of what you may say. It is ironic that the thing you did not want to manifest will indeed manifest, only making matters worse.

The principle is the same when you express your concern, anger, or frustration when your child has gone over a set boundary line. By disciplining your child in love, some measure of discomfort in some form or other may be the result, but setting the boundary brings peace to your child, knowing that you have acted in his or her best interest. Not taking corrective actions in love but exploding later instead brings only a feeling of insecurity and causes your child to question your love, which in itself results in further tantrums by the child and despair on your part.

Your true self as Divine will acknowledge that there is no need to fight your own battles. Do children feel that they have to fight to survive? I don't think so, for they know that their parents are there for them. Let's acknowledge that this may go against everything you have been taught. It's time to change the influence of Human and enter this place where somehow you know that everything is being taken care of because there is a belief in you, a knowing that someone is there for you, and that someone gladly takes all your cares and worries away from you. Take responsibility, yes, but give away the ownership. When you were a child, you had certain responsibilities in your home environment, but you rested in the knowledge that Mom and Dad took care of you. You belong to and are part of your spirit father and mother who take care of you. The spirit world is the real world, not the world that Human thinks is the real world. Divine needs a mind that is childlike, where there is no fear because of the knowing that you are loved and not alone.

When we learn to live in that awareness of our true selves, knowing that we are connected Spirit-to-spirit to our Creator, we allow the manifestation of love to work through us in any given situation. Because we are all unique, the manner in which this love flows through us differs from person to person.

Don't despair by thinking that changing everything is too difficult; it is so simple that you may miss it. The process involves a renewed relationship with your Creator, enabling you to become aware of this presence in you and around you. Again, this is so simple that it is almost difficult for us to accept, but I know that it will change who you think you are, which in turn will change your life.

Life's experiences either enhance or erode our self-esteem. When there is that observation that we do not measure up, we start believing that we lack value, and this is the start of the downward spiral where Human rules.

Here the judgement of ourselves can be like a fortress that imprisons us in our own world of worthlessness. Human continually reaffirms the lies that we are not good enough in many different situations, and we choose to believe this as the truth; as a result, our expectations are reaffirmed, which reinforce our feelings of worthlessness.

When you don't like yourself, others won't like you either, because they won't feel comfortable in your presence. The energy radiated will be self-centred because you will be so conscious of your own actions and words because of your insecurities that there will be no reaching out to others. That energy says that you don't want to hear others' problems—that you have enough of your own, so others should keep their distance. People will try to reason why they were not comfortable in your presence, and here the conscious mind tries to think of reasons they did not like you. In doing this, you are labelled, perhaps considered insincere, for example, so you withdraw even more from society. The fact of the matter is that you continue to experience people pushing you away because of your insecurities, which only strengthens Human's lies that you need to protect yourself even more because people are out there to hurt you. And so the cycle repeats itself.

Get to that place where you say that that's enough of this misery. I would urge you to practise meditation, to be still, to start listening to that voice in your inner core that says you are all good and all will be well with you because you are not alone. Take responsibility for your magnificence and be forceful in silencing Human and the rot that emanates from this source.

Don't listen to the madness of Human when it tries to persuade you that by saying sorry, you would be confirming that you are inferior to the person you are apologising to. Saying sorry comes from a place of strength and is the Divine you. It creates intimacy and openness. Strive for this, as it will bring you freedom.

Psychotherapist Nathaniel Branden, PhD, defines self-esteem as "the disposition to experience oneself as being incompetent to cope with the basic challenges of life and of being worthy of happiness."

What is happening here is that you are not able to love yourself because of the role Human is playing in your life. Not loving yourself puts you in a place where your ability to love unconditionally is weakened, and the resultant energy emanating from you will push those closest to you away because you will show a lack of compassion and kindness. Maybe none is deserved but should still be shown because this is how the Divine in you loves.

The truth of the matter is that in your uniqueness, you have qualities like no one else, qualities that can allow people to enjoy your presence and benefit from those qualities. Don't cheat the world of your magnificence. The Divine in you is standing by to serve those who cross your path, to bring a smile to a face, to make someone who is not feeling good about themselves to feel special, even if it is for a brief moment. This is the truth, yet Human may be screaming in your head right now that you have no value. It is time for you to shout back at Human to shut up. Enough lies and mistrust—enough hurting yourself and those closest to you.

I would encourage you to find something to do for someone else, no matter how small it is, for this takes the focus off yourself and builds up your self-image, knowing that you are contributing to the well-being of others and allowing Divine to rule. Give others the benefit of the doubt. Stop judging others and yourself because as you refrain from this habit, you will begin to see others as the magnificent people they are, even with their faults, and as you do this, your own opinion of yourself will improve. Up to now, the judgement you have imposed on others comes back to you, making you feel less of the person you want to be. And so the cycle of poor self-esteem continues.

PART 2:
CHANGING
EVERYTHING

There needs to be an awakening of our spirits (Divine) to the ways of our Creator. We need to grasp that our true selves are love, and with the power of love, your world will change. Human will make every effort to prevent you from entering this place of love, this kingdom of God, if you will. You may find yourself procrastinating in your plans to meditate in order to bring about the changes in thought patterns, so I will encourage you to be aware of Human and to make the free-will choice to allow quality time for yourself. Human will say that your time is needed for other things—how can you be so selfish? The fact is that not making time for yourself is being selfish, as you will be a far better person to those around you when you are at peace with yourself.

Living in the present moment enables you to operate from a place of love, whereas certain thoughts may well disable this process. Don't allow past or future thoughts to pre-empt any situation; instead, allow your love to be present in the now, reflecting compassion, and patience that results from the love in you.

CHAPTER 7

Connecting with Your Creator

The connection with your Creator as spirit is the source from which your Divine, being your spirit, gets guidance and inspiration. It is this spirit-to-spirit connection which is needed for Divine to take its rightful place as the mindset, as the kingdom of God that is your true self. Divine brings a mindset that is the complete opposite of the ways of a Human mindset. I have mentioned a number of these, but let's look at some that I may not have covered.

Human mindset	Divine mindset
You push away the love that is there for you, that is around you.	You are fully aware of the love of others for you, and you nurture that love.
Fear of not being able to obtain what you want or need dominates your mind.	There is no fear, for there is an understanding that the universe will supply whatever you need.

Financial lack consumes you, and hence the financial flow to you is restricted in some way. You work harder and harder and seem to get nowhere.	You know that money is your friend and will come generously into your life. You are able to receive money to facilitate your purpose of making your life matter.
You don't believe that you deserve more, and life becomes more about survival than a journey that can be enjoyed.	There are no limits to your abundance. You find what you enjoy doing, and in this you find fulfilment.
You are not in a position to give supportive advice that will build up but rather you have this need to protect yourself rather than consider the needs of others, causing discord in your family and not helping the situation.	You are able to step back and assess a situation without preconceived ideas or agendas and in the *now* moment provide advice that will support and help the situation.
What can God do for me?	What can God do through me?

A renewed mindset will allow gratitude to become the order of the day, gratitude for each moment, for family and friends, for your body. The awareness of the impact your thoughts have on your world and those closest to you becomes paramount. Your true identity in Divine becomes a reality, and in this you find peace and the joy that comes with that, for you will experience a greater energy taking charge of your life.

Remember that those wrong beliefs about your identity embedded within your subconscious need to be deleted, and this can be done through a constant awareness of your true self. Remember the principle of childlikeness, where Mom and Dad were always there, and the peace and security that this gave you or would give you as a child. The same applies to every moment of your day in that you are not alone so there is no need to fear. Find ways to enhance this truth, such as daily meditation and reading sections of this book and any other books that speak truth to you. Find music that calms you and reaffirms the love of that someone else who may be with you. Listed below are some truths which you need to continually remind yourself of in order to direct you to that inner core within you, that consciousness of the spirit you.

You are not alone—I find this one of the most important truths eluding most of us. As soon as you feel alone, you are vulnerable to fear, doubt, and depression. The moment the realisation that you are never alone becomes firmly implanted in your subconscious mind through meditation and affirmations and any other means that works for you, your whole being comes into balance because you were made to know this. You were made as a spirit being by your Creator, for this Creator who is spirit made you as spirit so that there can be that fellowship, that relationship, that connection which in itself brings peace.

An important aspect that we somehow lose sight of is that this source within us wants the very best for us because this source loves us. This sources waits to respond and meet our desires.

A free-will decision is necessary to remember that a feeling of isolation and loneliness in your endeavours to change everything is not Divine. The truth is that you are not alone in your quest to change everything. Once again, Human will sabotage this action because Human bases its existence on separation, on being alone, and you need to remember this.

Forgiveness—Forgiveness is needed when you hold on to the thoughts of others who have wronged you. Here Human can take a firm foothold because the hurts caused by others can be all-consuming. You may well have all the reason in the world to see these people as your enemies, and the thought of annihilating them may give you a measure of pleasure. However, the focus here is on you, and the need to hit back consumes you and you only. For example, the other person has forgotten the incident and doesn't think about you, yet the incident can consume your mind, thereby elevating that person to almost a godly position in your head because your thoughts dwell almost exclusively on that person. Once again, being aware of what is happening brings you to a place of choice, and in that place you can make the free-will choice to let it go, releasing yourself from that person or persons. In this process, the mountain is moved and Divine rules.

The other all-important aspect is forgiving yourself. I have found that not doing so is the most powerful form of bondage, for want of a better word. Almost on a continual base, Human reminds you from that subconscious place in your mind that you are of little worth and that you have messed up, bringing much pain to others. This information stored in your subconscious mind prevents

Divine from being elevated to its rightful place within you. As soon as you start making any form of progress, Human will remind you of the past, and this pulls you back into your hole.

I want you to see what is happening here because you need to release yourself from this position. We have all made mistakes where we have been more focused on our own needs rather than considering the needs of others, especially those who have possibly trusted us to be there for them. I know this is not easy, but I want to encourage you to say sorry to those you have hurt if the situation allows it. Then let it go. Understand that this lack of forgiveness is limiting you in your effectiveness to be there for others, and in not getting to that place of forgiving yourself, you are fact being selfish, and this is where Human wants you to stay. Human's reasoning will be that it's safer to alienate yourself rather than expose yourself to further hurt and ridicule. Something in you will hold on to this thought because you want to see the other person suffer in some way. This is Human keeping you from discovering the I AM in you, that part of you that knows everything happens for a purpose. You will grow from your experiences or go around in circles because of them; the choice is yours.

Divine stands by waiting for you to get to that place where you see the folly in your holding on to the need to see those who have done you harm suffer in some way, making sure that they don't think that everything is now fine and dandy. You need to see the harm that you are bringing to yourself, the misery that will continue to stay with you, entrapping you in a world where joy and peace may be scarce.

Forgiveness is about you, not the other person. Forgiving is not condoning the actions of the offender. It is not making right what has been done to you. Forgiveness enables you to let go of the past. Letting go of the past sets you free from that data which would continually remind you of the harm done to you, and in this place, Divine can rule.

Let's look at some examples. Someone hurts you not so much physically but emotionally, which causes disappointment and feelings of rejection. I say to forgive him. You may say no way, that by treating him as though nothing has happened makes him feel that you are condoning his actions. This thinking is from Human because Human wants him to feel guilty and suffer in some way. Is this love? Is this Divine? I don't think so. I say to forgive him for two reasons. The first is because the pain he has caused you is a result of your own insecurities. This sounds harsh, but we need to get to a place where we stop trying to justify our own misery. The second is that he has judged you because of his own insecurities and issues, which is his Human. Don't allow the judgement of others to create negative energy in you, thereby blocking Divine. We have to get to a place where the judgement of others does not impact our self-worth. Yes, it hurts but dust yourself off and continue on your merry way. Your joy needs to be such that it overrides the judgement of others.

The bottom line is that when I am offended, I need to forgive, and I am only offended when Human rules in my mind. Think of that for a moment: you and I are only offended when we see ourselves as victims. As Divine, you cannot be a victim; the victim mentality comes from Human. Only Divine can forgive. Human hangs on to the offence, trying to justify the anger and misery it causes you. It's a choice again: Human or Divine.

Human causes your mind to be consumed by a world that consists only of you. Every thought is about you and how you are affected, how you are being treated, how hard you are working, how unfair life has treated you. This is a trap of Human and needs to be recognised as such.

Intimacy with your spouse or partner—Your commitment to your partner or spouse is where the tyre meets the tar. It is here where choices are made on a daily basis as to who rules your thoughts. A solid relationship manifests through love; an unstable relationship manifests Human. You are the one that must bring the changes required as you become aware of your true self, and that energy flowing from you will facilitate the change in your partner. That energy which is caring and kind when there are plenty of reasons not to show kindness is what brings about the change. Don't think that this change of energy will go unnoticed by your spouse.

Be sure to appreciate your partner. Put him or her on a pedestal in your mind,. See your children as the gifts they are. Human will come along and ask how you can be kind to your child when she has given you so much grief, not respecting you and so on. Once again, Human causes your thoughts to revolve around you, and this is the trap. Remember that offence only comes from Human, and that offence comes when you are not grasping that you are Divine. Start seeing those closest to you as the spirit beings of love that they are, just as you need to see yourself as a spirit being of love. This will enable you to move away from the judgements of others and yourself.

Be transparent to your spouse or partner—Be prepared to expose yourself because this is not a characteristic of Human. Don't say that you are fine when you are not fine. If you are not fine but don't feel like discussing it then and there, then say so. In doing this, you may feel that you are risking vulnerability, but that is good. Say when you are feeling lonely or are fearful about something. You will find a release from having to pretend, and most importantly, you are encouraging intimacy, which is the real Divine you. By saying that you are fine when you are not is Human building one of those walls which keeps you away from those who simply want to care. It is not about solving the problems; it's about caring. Allow others to care and to receive their kindness. You can make the choice to do this. Don't allow Human to push those closest to you away, for you will subconsciously do this, not realising the harm and misery that you are bringing upon yourself.

Live in gratitude—Counting your blessings is something that Human does not do; living in gratitude requires letting go of cynicism. Distrusting others' motives and exercising control is what Human thrives on. After all, your Human has perfected your walls of fear to supposedly protect you. Suddenly being grateful for life and so many facets of it poses a high risk for Human's position because then all the emotional drama and the need to be in control and to manipulate are exposed as a grand fiction.

Make a list of all the facets of life that you should be grateful for, such as your body, even if it is not perfect according to your point of view; your health, even if that is not perfect; your friends and loved ones; water and food; clothes; and those things only known by you. Be grateful for every now moment and see your world change.

Don't always strive to get your way—Rise above the temptation to prove someone else wrong. See the folly in this and the lack of fulfilment it brings. Human tries to convince you that your way is the only way. Once again, Human is centred all on you, and you cannot be the centre when your way is not seen as the high way. Stand back and see what is happening; this is not Divine operating, only the madness of Human.

Say sorry—What is important is to get your mind to a place where you can sincerely and simply apologise when you have acted or behaved in a negative manner. In doing this, you are exposing Human, thereby breaking down the attempts of Human to keep the walls up.

Be positive—If you believe that people will be nice to you, they will. See the good in others and they will see the good in you. See the bad in others and they will see the bad in you. Human is negative; therefore, don't justify being negative. There is always a positive aspect. There is always hope. There is always something to be grateful for. Don't look for what is wrong; look for what is right. I know I seem to be preaching here, but these must be the reminders, the red lights that say to you, "Hello, it's Human here."

Don't be offended—We have looked at offence, but it is a key in ridding ourselves from the rule of Human. Be aware that offence comes only when you question your own identity. You can be offended by a remark which was said simply to make conversation. You can be offended when someone is late in picking you up, perhaps because you feel that he or she doesn't care enough or respect you enough to make sure to be there on time. The underlying aspect of offence is that your thoughts are saying that people don't care, even those who are your closest allies. This is the madness of Human. Recognise it for what it is. It has only brought unhappiness to your life, and in order for change to come, you must change your thoughts regarding your worth. When you do this and start forgiving yourself, believing that those closest to you do love and care for you, you will start seeing the truth, which is that you are cared for and loved.

Refrain from any form of judgement—We have discussed judgement, but it is also a major obstacle in our quest for Divine to rule. Judgment brings separation, and we know that Human thrives on this. Stop judging yourself, for it separates you from Divine. Stop judging others, for it separates you from them, and often it's those closest to you whom you are judging. Have a point of view because that allows room for change. There must not be an I-am-right-and-you-are-wrong point of view. Both parties should have a point of view but no more than that.

Many people have gone through dark places and have looked back to say that those have actually been their finest hours. Dark places changed their lives as they called out to God and found that he was right there, or they have found that inner strength to show gratitude in a seemingly hopeless situation, and in this the power was there, the belief was there, to know that they were not alone.

When we can see that everything that comes our way has a purpose, we are operating in Divine. Human will play no part in this and disagree because then it is difficult to justify the complaining and on-going judgment. Human raises its fist to the darkness and curses the event and this only brings on more darkness.

On the other hand, Divine will enable you to receive comfort during times of heartache, and although there will not be an answer to the *why*, you will find peace. I urge you to take hold of the truth that all is well in your life right now, regardless of the heartache you may be experiencing.

Love sees beauty in all things, and as you become aware of your divine nature as the true you, you realise that beauty and truth are synonymous. You need to see yourself as the limitless abundance that you are. You are more spirit than flesh, and spirit has no lack and no end, much like the universe itself. Grasp that truth of your abundance and discard Human, who will be shouting from the sidelines to look at the realities of what you lack. I would remind Human that the lack is the doubt and fear caused by a mindset not aware of your true self and that is about to change. Remember that you will not be able to see outside of you what you cannot see inside of you. You will not see beauty and love if you don't love yourself. You are the abundance you seek, you are the love you long for, you are the peace.

Be honest with yourself in how your mind is interpreting events and make the free-will choice to stop listening to Human which will sabotage any lasting happiness in your life. Some examples:

"They must change so that my opinion is enforced, so that I am right."

"I need to judge so that I can prove I am right."

"I must hold on to my self-imposed limitation; it is safer."

"Life is not good; it's a struggle."

"What about this awareness does not work?"

Let's look at some of the scriptures about Peter and how he seemed to struggle with Human, but then overcomes by Divine ruling in his life. Here Peter reacts to what Jesus says: "From that time on Jesus began to explain to his disciples that he must go to Jerusalem and suffer many things at the hands of the elders, chief priests and teachers of the law, and that he must be killed and on the third day be raised to life. Peter took him aside and began to rebuke him. 'Never, Lord!' he said. 'This shall never happen to you!' Jesus turned and said to Peter, 'Get behind me, Satan! You are a stumbling block to me; you do not have in mind the things of God, but the things of men'" (Matthew 16:21-23 NIV).

Here Jesus refers to Human as the things of men and Divine as the things of God. Meaning well, Peter cannot accept that any harm can come to Jesus and says this cannot be. What is happening here is that Peter is missing the very essence of Jesus's purpose. Peter's thoughts are in line with his Human, focusing on the fact that he did not intend for things to work out this way. Peter means well, but he is not seeing the bigger picture, which was that Jesus would die for you and me. With a Human mindset we will not see the bigger picture for our lives and fall into the same trap as Peter.

Luke 22:62 tells us that Peter went and wept bitterly after Jesus looked at him after he had denied three times that he knew him. I am sure that Jesus still looked at him with compassion and mercy. Jesus knew the real Peter, just as he knows the real you and I, and he could see ahead to when this man Peter, full of his spirit, full of Divine, would be prepared to also lay down his life. What happens to Peter? Here it becomes evident that the Human that there may have been in Peter in fearing for his life and denying that he knew Jesus is replaced by Divine over time where he is prepared to sacrifice his life, as history has it that Peter willingly laid down his life a few years later.

Life comes along and convinces us that we need to protect ourselves and take control because no one else will, when the truth is we need to get back to that childlike mindset of trusting in the love of our Creator to supply the abundance of life that is ours. Giving ourselves over to love is not difficult, but losing that control is difficult for Human. Without the awareness of this struggle within you to lose control, you are not able to make the choice to surrender that control.

CHAPTER 8

The Man Jesus

Let's look at this man Jesus. Don't see Jesus as representing some form of religion but rather a means to help you in finding Divine. It is important that we look at the man Jesus to grasp his purpose and learn what his presence on earth may have accomplished.

We need to grasp the never ending love of our Creator and Jesus does enable us to do that to some extent when we look at the words recorded that this man spoke. For me Jesus reflects the heart of our Creator; in this, he is one of the closest persons to reflect the nature of our Divine. If God created us, we must then be like him. You might ask if that doesn't make us gods, and I'd have to say that yes, I see it no other way. There is no end to us, just as there is no end to our Creator. We have the ability to create our own lives and the energy that will radiate from them.

Jesus reflects God, and in this we obtain a measure of understanding of God. The name Jesus, or Yeshua, is also referred to as Emmanuel, meaning 'God with us'. The scriptures tell us that Jesus was "God manifest in the flesh" (1 Timothy 3:16).

On a number of occasions, Jesus said to different people he was meeting for the first time, "Your sins are forgiven." How can this be? We need to stop here for a moment and grasp what this means. I can only forgive someone who has wronged me; I can't forgive someone who has wronged someone else. Jesus can then only forgive our sin if we have sinned against him. It therefore becomes evident that the wrongs we have done (which I would interpret as a wrong heart attitude; even though we are aware of this, we have not been prepared to take up our responsibility to change) have been against Jesus. Is he not therefore in all of us? Is it not his love that is wounded when we choose not to change but rather to operate in our own selfish self-centred worlds?

With a mindset of Divine, are we not finding a little of our Creator's love, a little of his power and a little of his mind? As you find God in a more real way, you find love. God is love, and that love has the power to change everything. We cannot love unless we have a source of love in us. We all fall short in this area, but it is a process. Remember that life needs to be a process of rediscovering your true self so that in this you can operate with a mindset of Divine, which in turn leads you to a full life which is enjoyed, not a struggle. As we receive this love, we are then able to love others unconditionally.

I want you to visualise yourself walking on a beach. The sun is starting to appear over the horizon. There are clouds in the distance over the sea, with the sun piercing through the clouds. There is no wind, and it is warm. You have no pain in your body, but there is a brokenness within you and you are feeling alone, wishing that you could feel the joy of sharing this moment with someone who could understand you and be caring in a genuine way.

> Imagine you are walking barefoot on the sand, you find a man walking next to you who knows your name, but for some reason, you are not startled, and you feel safe in his presence. As he walks alongside you, somehow you feel that this man, for a reason that is not clear to you, has known you your whole life and genuinely cares for your well-being.
>
> He asks you why you are troubled, and you reply too harshly by saying, "Why do you care?"
>
> His answer: "I made you to be my companion, I lost you, needed to sacrifice my life for you to get you back, and now you are again mine." You are overwhelmed by a sense of love and compassion emanating from this man, a strength and confidence in his words that make you feel safe.
>
> When you ask him why he had to sacrifice his life for you, he answers, "To enable you to be part of my kingdom." You realise that you don't need to understand this right now,

but that somehow it is the truth and you are overwhelmed by gratitude for his knowing you.

He says, "Remember that what I see in you is more important than what others think of you, including yourself, and what I see in you is someone I have wonderfully made with no lack, limitation, or disease, someone that I love with no conditions attached. Someone with the potential to impact lives in a way like no other because of your uniqueness."

He explains to you that you need to depend on him as a small child would depend on his or her mother and father, allowing him to be part of your life so that you never feel alone again. When you look again, you can't see him, but somehow you feel he is still there.

Become aware of the source of love in you, which is there to make your life matter. It is difficult to understand the spiritual world, but once again, be childlike in your approach and embrace this love that you find in you and for you.

It is important to find a quiet and secluded place so that you can relax and be conscious of the here and now, completely unconcerned about both the past and the future, allowing your mind to be still. Try to do this every day for at least half an hour. Do this through meditation that works for you.

Remember that you are peace and you are joy, and as you learn to be aware of this, you will only attract smiles and friendship throughout your day. Understand the power of the energy that surrounds you. It impacts the hardest of hearts and allows God to create your world through you.

Make sure you find time to meditate, pray and do whatever you want to do. Don't allow these breaks to bring guilt because of all your other responsibilities. Once again, this is Human not wanting to lose control, so be sure to recognise this. This may not be easy, for Human wants you to believe that you need to keep busy, maybe even subconsciously creating a level of stress in your daily life because that it what you believe you deserve. Recognise the mind of Human and know that it is not the truth.

CHAPTER 9

You Are Not Alone

We have touched on this, but because of the importance of it, I would like us to focus on this truth some more. The reality is that we have an energy force around us and in us, waiting to be accessed through our Divine. When there is no awareness of Divine or Human, then the absence of that awareness allows no choice to be made, and when no choice is made Human unfortunately will be there as your default mindset. On the other hand, Sam is there as your teacher, reminding you of the presence of this unseen energy that is the I AM in you, namely your Divine.

A tool to experience more of Divine in your life is to make the choice to be aware of the love of Divine in you for others. As you become aware of the I AM in you and make the choice to give of this love, mercy, forgiveness and kindness, with no judgement to others, all those things will flow back to you. It's like the waves that push out onto the sand from the rich source of the sea and then rush back from where they came. You have this unlimited source which gives out and then comes back to you, ensuring that your source never runs dry.

Do you have a dream? If not, the reason may be that you don't feel that there is any purpose to life and therefore no reason to dream. There is no purpose to a dream when you feel that you are on your own and know that on your own, your dreams stand little chance of materialising. On the other hand, if you realise that you are not alone and have access to an unlimited source, then dreams can become a reality. Human is quick to say to you that you need to be realistic, that you have your limitations that failure will make you feel even worse than you feel right now so this becomes your comfort zone, even if it is a miserable place.

It's time to recognise who you are not. It's time to see what Human is doing to you, because Human needs to be fed, and Human is fed through your wrong beliefs which form part of your false identity. Be aware of these kinds of thoughts emanation from your Human mindset. Be aware of this lie: "I am alone and nobody cares." I realise that it is easy to write these words, but believe me when I say that your Creator does care, and that it's Human blocking the peace you long for. The truth of an omnipresence constantly with you must form part of your subconscious mind so that regardless of circumstances, you will automatically be able to laugh in the face of the mountains that may want to loom up ahead of you. And as you do this, you speak to them and they move because the words you speak are not emanating from Human but from Divine, with the full backing of God, who made the universe. Grasp your magnificence, your likeness to your Creator. This is faith, knowing that you are not alone and grasping as best as you know how the magnitude of the power of your support base.

This God of love in you removes guilt and shame as you grasp the truth that you are all good and not bad, which helps you to find Divine rather than Human, which has a way of convincing you that you are not all good. Love does not judge, and for this reason, God will not judge you. Remember Human judges all the time, including yourself, saying to you that you are not all good which brings no peace, while Divine will not judge you or anyone else.

Our minds need to be renewed; there needs to be that change in mindset. We know that some people are prepared to die for an ideal, for what they perceive as a godly action that will bring some benefit to themselves but certainly not for other people. Jesus' story is that he sacrificed himself to save others, not to benefit himself in any way. He dies for you and me so that we could have access to the spirit world of love enabling us to rid ourselves of any control by Human.

> As human beings we all want to be happy and free from misery . . . we have learned that the key to happiness is inner peace. The greatest obstacles to inner peace are disturbing emotions such as anger, attachment, fear and suspicion, while love and compassion and a sense of universal responsibility are the sources of peace and happiness.
>
> (Dalai Lama)

These are great words. What causes the disturbing emotions? Only the lies of Human, who through life's experiences and the way we have interpreted these experiences, convince ourselves that we are alone and not worthy of any form of happiness because we are bad. Dear reader, this madness must end. You are wonderfully made, and I want you to feel that love around you right now. Feel its embrace and know that all will be well, that you have a friend, your Creator, who made you as an integral part of the big picture, too big for you to see, just as the universe is too big for you to see. Your purpose is to discover that limitlessness of your true self and see how you can make your life matter by being there for others in some way, living out your creativity and the talents that are in you. Human may say that you have none, but believe me that that is a lie.

When you change your mindset to be childlike, there is a constant awareness of a spirit father or mother; however, you prefer to see God, where you nurture thoughts of trust, of forgiveness, of love just as a child would have for his or her loving parents.

A young child does not compare himself with others. Life comes along and starts that process of measuring ourselves against others. We take part in races, competitions, and exams; and the mindset of "How do I measure up to others?" begins. Imagine no more comparisons and measuring yourself against others. Imagine if you could grasp the truth that you as a spirit being need no improvements because you are unique and wonderfully made. Most importantly is the realisation that to enter this mindset of childlikeness requires Divine to rule. Therefore, the key is to develop the awareness of your true identity as the spirit being that you are, which has a relationship with your Creator, bringing you the realisation that you are never alone. In this childlike place, you then experience the expectation of miracles. "What else is possible?" can be asked, knowing that anything is possible.

I want to encourage you in the knowledge that I have experienced miracle upon miracle in my daily life as I have learnt to be more aware of the childlikeness within me when it comes to trusting as a child would trust. Philosopher Mencius Chinen said the following: "Great is the man who has not lost his childlike heart." The idea is not to shirk responsibilities, but rather to find ways to interject fun into your everyday life together with a knowing that you are backed up, as it were by an all-powerful, loving, caring God and in this place miracles can take place.

Even when they do disappoint, children know that their parents love them, with no conditions attached. Even if they step out of line at times and have to bear the consequences of that, it will not change their relationship with Mom and Dad, for that simply cannot change. Their mothers and fathers will always be their parents; nothing can take that away. The chances are pretty good that you will be the cause of some strife and pain and may well need to bear the consequences in some form, but that does not lessen God's love for you. You don't need to do anything to deserve His love, just as a child does not have to do anything to deserve the love of a parent.

I know there is a God of love, and I am fortunate enough to experience that love, even though I wrestle with my Human, with its self-pity, selfishness, greed, and whatever else chooses to appear from seemingly nowhere. For the most part, I am able to be aware of this and choose not to operate within this negative energy. I know that this is not the real me and therefore make the choice not to feed this other side of me but rather let it starve by not dwelling on the thoughts generated by that side of me being Human. In this awareness, that energy leaves me because it has nothing to hang on to for its further development and nourishment.

We know that we are not alone, yet terrible things happen to good people who were also not alone. For example, why does an innocent girl get brutally raped and murdered? Why does a tornado rip through a peaceful countryside, causing the death of dear people? Why does an aeroplane go down, killing hundreds of people? We can't claim to understand these things.

Even though we know there is a God of love, we also know that there are millions of people going hungry and having little hope, to say the least. Maybe my thoughts about this will help you grasp that somehow we all create our world collectively, and as we all strive to be more of our true selves, the world will become a better place.

Our Humans, which we are all feeding, all create energy, and this energy is destructive. Let's take an example of lust and poor self-worth. I was listening to a programme where a couple brutally murdered and raped a twelve-year-old girl. This disturbed me, and I was desperate for some kind of answer. I will try to explain as best as I can the answer that came to me although and I am not saying that I have covered all the factors at work.

The man in the story was feeding his lust by wanting to have sex with a virgin. He told his partner that if she helped him achieve this, he would always be there for her. He was aware of her desire to be loved and thereby manipulates her to be part of his scheme. She makes the choice to feed her selfish desires of belonging to someone regardless of the cost. They followed a young girl on her bicycle and stopped her by asking her a question; then they abducted her, raping and stabbing her. She was the epitome of beauty, intelligence, kindness, and everything a parent could be proud of. Why did she have to die a terrible death?

We live in a world where everything is energy, either destructive or creative. The lust in that man was a form of destructive energy from hundreds or maybe thousands of Humans, which then manifests through a man who was willing to feed his own lust to such an extent that he was prepared to sacrifice a life to meet his own needs. The woman was also consumed by a destructive energy emanating from many other individuals who believe in their own unworthiness, and in an effort to feel worthy by gaining favour with her partner at whatever cost, she justified in her own selfish mind that it was worth being part of this hideous deed, creating further pain and suffering to meet her own needs. She was so blinded by her selfishness that she could not see that she was only going to make herself feel more unworthy, to a point where she would self-destruct to a point of no return. There must be a point of no return regarding one's soul when a person allows their mind to get to such a place where they can carry out hideous crimes to innocent children who plead for their lives.

You may then ask why God allows this. The answer is that he is not part of this. He has created the spiritual laws which enable us to be the creators of the world we live in. We choose joy or misery, we create the world we live in we choose Human or Divine to rule. In these choices, either destructive or creative energy emanates from us; either way, based on our choices, there are pre-set outcomes according to spiritual laws. Destructive energy will always lean towards death and destruction, while creative energy is life, a connection with your Creator and the abundance of life. The more we all unify in our endeavours not to feed our Humans, which will strive to survive by being fed thoughts on evil ideas, sexual lust, theft, murder, adultery, greed, evil, deceit, envy, pride, and so on, the less destructive energy we will create, hence a less violent world. We need to be aware that the destructive energy emanating from our Humans can bring suffering of some kind to other innocent people, and not only ourselves. On the other hand, the more we feed our Divines, the more love and creative energy will be in the world, bringing peace and joy not only to ourselves but also to others, through people's acts of love and kindness.

What about the precious people who have had to suffer in some way or lose their lives for the sake of this destructive energy force that is sourced from within us? It is almost as if they were too good to be part of this world. It was out of their control. I do believe that they find themselves in a wonderful place. As the heavens are too much for us to grasp, so is this place. Families experiencing the loss of these loved ones and the incomprehensive pain that goes with it either feed their Humans or their Divines, meaning that they either become more of their true selves or less of their true self. For the most part, I have seen these dear folks get stronger and find Divine in their heartache.

I do hope that for those people who have had to experience this kind of pain in losing loved ones, where there may be a measure of anger towards God for their grief, that this will bring an understanding that God is not part of these acts. We are unable to see the bigger picture now, but one day it will become clear. God is still in complete control and I urge you not to doubt that. The change in mindset is our choice, regardless of our circumstances.

When we choose to feed our Humans continually, we not only set ourselves up for hardship and pain but also create our own hell for this dimension and possibly the next dimension. We may find ourselves in a place where there is no presence of love, only fear of some kind, because this is what we have chosen, a place with no spiritual connection to God. Again, God didn't create this place; we did. Do you really think a God of love would create a place of pain and suffering? I don't think so. We create our own hell by possibly finding ourselves in a place where there is no love and no God—just more of the misery we created in this dimension. Perhaps we keep coming back if we have not grasped the fundamentals of love, and only once we have will we enter the presence of God. Who knows? What is important is that we have only ourselves to blame if we are not in this place of love and the abundance that comes with love. I do believe that heaven is a place created by God for those leaving this dimension, for those who have chosen to experience an awareness of love, bringing a measure of caring and comfort to others by listening, supporting, and caring through their Divine.

Love without actions is dead; standing up for those who cannot defend themselves is also love. Love does not look the other way when the weak are being molested. If we all stood up in unity through Divine, exposing the Human that rules in so many and the misery this causes, the world would be a much better place with far less suffering.

PART 3:
THE ROAD
AHEAD

In this final section of the book, I would like to reaffirm some of the important aspects of getting ourselves to a place where Divine rules, where life is good, and where love flows from a never-ending source from within.

CHAPTER 10

The Wonderful You

Your spirit-to-spirit communication, namely your spirit (Divine) and that of your Creator who is spirit, needs to take place in your daily life. Just as we can't expect to a have a fulfilling relationship with our partners or spouses without spending time with them, the same goes for the relationship with our Creator.

Your self-worth governs every area of your life, and what you believe about yourself will be reflected in your life. Human will only allow you to attain a level of happiness that you have set for yourself in your subconscious mind, based on what you believe you deserve. As soon as you start exceeding this level of happiness Human will find a way to bring you back to your more than likely unhappy state. This can occur by you starting an argument with your spouse for no real reason. Human sets limits for your happiness, wealth, health and relationships. Be aware of this because in that awareness you will be able to make the choice for Divine to rule, allowing you to surpass those default settings you have set for yourself based on your self worth. The realisation that you, a wonderful being, made in the image of your Creator who wants only the very best for you, needs to become a reality without losing site that the same applies for those around you.

Past data in your subconscious mind based on your beliefs associated with your identity, will cause blockages in your efforts for Divine to come through allowing you to break free from those limits you have set for yourself.

These memories are deleted as an awareness of your true self-worth as Divine becomes known through your spirit-to-spirit communication with your Creator. Your subconscious mind will over time store the new data concerning your newfound beliefs in who you are, and this data will override the old data simply because the new data is truth. The old data was based on information gathered over years of living an illusion of who you thought you were (Human) based on your life's experiences.

Many people don't understand why they can't experience the breakthroughs they so desire no matter how hard they try. You begin to think you are 'cursed' or that the universe is against you in some way. The answer lies in knowing your greatness as a spirit being, where unconditional love is found with no judgement.

Life and the abundance of it cannot be found in Human. As you operate from a mindset of Divine you are aware of your true identity as a spirit being, your thoughts will be operating in the now from a baseline of love, not allowing past data to pre-empt any situations.

You need to feel the joy that you would experience as if you had already received what you desire, as in the spiritual world, what you believe has already manifested. The problem is that we say we believe, but we don't really believe unless we can experience the positive emotion that goes with that belief, as if it had already occurred. This creative power rests in you.

Feel good about who you are and what you mean to your Creator and know that the universe is behind you; this God, this Yahweh, this all-encompassing love is there for you to embrace. Feel the love that God has for you, not because of anything you have done but because you belong to the universe; you are part of God. As you become more aware of this presence you will experience the whole universe being behind you in your endeavours to attain a life that matters by being able to live out your true self and the talents that are part of that true self. You will find that everything to do with your purpose will be drawn to you as you radiate positive energy from within you. This enables the Creator of all things to create your world as you would believe it to be. You have that power; your world is who you are, so focus daily on the real you and who you are. The days of a mindset based on Human must go. Be aware of its negative influence on your thoughts, as Human is part of you and will not disappear. However, its influence on your thoughts will become less significant as you spend time meditating on the I AM in you.

There is joy in understanding your position as a spirit being made in God's image. There is joy in knowing that there is no need to protect yourself, for you are permanently in a place of protection when you believe in your true identity, the real you, the Divine you. We read in the scriptures "The joy of the Lord is our strength." (Nehemiah 8:10). The Hebrew word for strength is 'ma owz', meaning a fortified place, a place of refuge, a stronghold, a shelter, a place of safety. This place of joy requires no energy from us to protect ourselves, for we are already in a place where no harm can come to us, so there is simply no need for any form of protection, especially from Human. Remember that Human has always made you believe that you are the victim and that you need to protect yourself because you are not in a safe place. This brings that feeling of vulnerability of being alone. Remind yourself that this is a lie emanating from Human.

There is so much more, and we need to tap into this oasis of abundant living, which I see as not necessarily material things but being the joy that comes when your activities or work revolves around making use of the talents that have been given to you. Because of our individuality, we all experience these things differently so run with your spirit and the power that is within you. My desire is for you to get to a place where Human is out of the way in order for you to start your own personal journey with your Creator the way it is meant to be so that you can receive love from those around you and from the Spirit of God in you.

We are all unique spirit beings, and the result of this is that we all have different experiences in our relationship with God. This experience is personal and different for each one of us because of our individuality.

Love is the only way in bringing about peace and joy. So love yourself and be prepared to love those who are not lovable. Stop finding fault as Human does; instead, see the goodness in others, as it is there somewhere. See others as the spirit beings that they are, regardless of the Human mindset that you may see in them.

Believe that the spirit of God in you will strengthen you and guide you in every situation. If your spouse has hurt you deeply, I urge you to forgive, understanding that he or she have their own struggles with Human. Remember that there is no judgement; there are no winners and no losers.

CHAPTER 11

Meditation

Meditation needs to be practised daily to enable you to quieten your thoughts and in that quietness experience the real you, where peace, love and comfort can be found. In my efforts to be still, I will at times put my fingers in my ears so that I can hear my breathing. Imagine that the Spirit of your Creator in you is closer than the breath you can hear. Know that you are not alone. Let there be an awareness of this limitless power and abundance of every kind within you; above all, be aware of the peace that is that quietness itself. The concept is for there to be a spirit-to-spirit connection because in this the mind is renewed as you start realising that the whole universe is waiting to make your life all good, but it needs your consent.

Think of what is resting heavily on your mind and then picture what a different scenario would be like. How would you feel if you were freed from this? Don't be concerned as to how this could come about—just enjoy the freedom and feel the joy as if what was resting heavily on your mind is not there. Believe that it will be so. Spend time being quiet in the presence of your Creator and listen. Remember, the answers are in you.

Meditation is entering into a sacred space of quietness where that very quietness becomes tangible; it becomes the source of love that flows in you and through you. In this space, all uncertainty in the truth of who you are as a spirit being melts away. In this space, let gratitude well up in you, giving thanks for all you have, including the challenges. In this, you open the door to allow the power, love, and confidence to flow in you and through you.

Meditation is a personal thing in that because we are unique, we will find through trial and error a particular kind of meditation that works for us. However, here are some guidelines.

For the beginning of the day, try this. Control your breathing and breathe deeper than usual. Breathing has a way of controlling the mind and emotions so breathe deeply, putting your feet firmly on the floor if sitting in a chair. Bring your consciousness to a place of quiet listening. Say to yourself, "Today I have more than enough for every obstacle that crosses my path. Love, power, and a sound mind will operate through me this day as Divine rules. Each thought will be fused with love. Thoughts of lack of some kind may enter my mind this day, but I will remember that abundance is mine; there is no limit to anything within the kingdom of God. I will be alive and aware of each moment of this day, knowing that this energy in me, this energy of love in me, ensures that everything works in my favour and nothing is able to stand in the way of this energy, even though it may seem otherwise."

Controlling your breathing is a sure way to control your stress levels. Try it for yourself and you will notice a difference. Feel your lungs filling with air and then exhale. Practise quieting your mind. Other thoughts will come, but see those thoughts passing by without your partaking in them. Create space for the quietness; that quietness and stillness is the place where you get in touch with your inner core, where truth is found, truth in the knowledge that all is well.

Let's be honest: at times, you may feel that all hell is breaking loose and fear has gripped you. Here the old identity (Human) is trying to raise its head causing you to feel alone and possibly abandoned. Meditate with the awareness of the truth that you have a source within you that created the world and everything in it including the mountains.

Know that Human will not want you to meditate, for this venture into a new dimension of peace will disrupt the status quo. This something inside of you will again sabotage what is good for you. You may even feel that venturing into unknown places of your mind is something that you would prefer not to do. These thoughts would be from Human, for you cannot fear something that you don't know; you only fear leaving that which you do know, and this is how Human tries to keep you from moving away or out of your comfort zone, therefore recognise the source of these thoughts.

Human will try to prevent the loss of the known because venturing into unknown territory needs to be avoided at all costs. The reasons for this are that the old familiar control mechanisms of Human may not work in a different place, or in a different mindset. Human will hang on to the familiar even though it's not a good place; at least it is known. Awareness of this will help you make the choice to venture into unfamiliar territory, a place where you release control over to your Creator a place where your true self is found.

As you progress with your meditation time, you will find that you want certain things around you to assist in getting yourself to a place of quietness. Meditation is a form of action; it is not simply a distraction from your surroundings. It helps you stop worrying because Divine is found in that quiet place. That awakening comes about through that spirit-to-spirit awareness, where the truth of your Creator's purpose for you, which is to experience life and the abundance of it through making your life matter (which at the end of the day is doing those things that you enjoy doing because you were created to do those things); that is the real you. It is those things that make you feel alive. Because of our uniqueness, how we make life matter is a discovery in itself—and a personal one for each of us. Don't think for one moment that you are not good enough to make your life matter. That is only Human trying to stop you from venturing outside your comfort zone; trying to protect you from further disappointment which needs to be seen as a hic-up rather than something to avoid at all costs.

Jesus said, "The kingdom of God is within you" (Luke 17:21). In meditation, we enter that kingdom, that Divine place where no protection is needed because you are safe within the kingdom. You don't seek safety when you are in a safe or secured area where no unwanted individuals can enter. It's when you are outside that secured area that you are vulnerable, and because Human has no kingdom, you feel that you need to protect yourself every moment of the day from hurt, disappointment, judgement, fear, insecurity, and all those things that make life miserable.

Meditation is the science, as it were, of getting the mind, body, and spirit to work together, bringing about a balance where the truth of your true identity becomes a reality. Meditation helps you detect what changes need to be made in your thought processes, and you need to commit to making those changes. Meditation becomes an effective tool in finding peace, which also comes about through a change in your own energy as you choose to listen to your inner core by operating from a place of limitlessness, where there is no end to the source of life that is Yahweh, that place of compassion and love. In this place, you change the way you interact with the world, and this you will begin to see quiet clearly by the different way people respond to you.

I would encourage you to read about different forms of meditation or methods, changing them from time to time to see what works best for you.

For change to come about, you need to change, so when Human says you are wasting your time with meditating, remind Human that up to now, there have not been too many ground breaking ideas coming from that side.

Prayer is a form of meditation so press forward in building a relationship with your Creator through spirit-to-spirit contact. See yourself as a sponge absorbing the living water from that limitless source found within the kingdom of your Creator—that place where there is joy. In that joy, you will find strength and healing for your body. You will find favour of every kind.

The world is a magical and divine place, but most of the time we only see the deadlines and the bills that need to be paid. There is more, believe me, and that more is found in you.

CHAPTER 12

Conclusion

As we end this short journey on paper, I do want to believe that you will be starting your own journey with a renewed mindset, a mindset that will be more aware of the bigger power within you—a power of love that will create your own world and change everything in it. The change will come about through Sam as that awareness of Human and Divine that abide in you. An awareness of the sabotage capabilities of Human, sabotaging what is good for you, trying to keep you within those limits you have set for yourself around the abundance of life. An awareness of Divine being that part of you that is unconditional love, a side of you that cares for others and yourself, always showing mercy. An acceptance of Human is necessary, as Human is part of you and has a role to play while knowing that Divine is your true identity and needs to rule through your own free-will choice.

The role of Human and the misery it has caused will cease as it becomes subservient to Divine being your true self. Your Divine will take you on a journey building a relationship with your Creator. There is simply nothing impossible for you to ask for when it comes to knowing who you are as a spirit being.

Your purpose for life is to express the I AM in you and in this manifest Divine through love, compassion, forgiveness, and joy. The purpose of this book is to set a platform for you to commence your own journey of discovery through a renewed awareness of Divine in you as your true self. You will become aware of the daily miracles, realising that nothing is coincidental. You will discover that for the most part, your true self has remained dormant all these years simply because you have unknowingly allowed life as you have understood it, to block the flow of your Divine through the lack of awareness of Human and the destructive influence that Human has been having on your life. Remember that Human seeks acceptance and fears not being liked. Divine, on the other hand, knows that love is acceptance and fear can only manifest when you think that you will not be able to attain something you need. Divine is complete and needs nothing.

You will become aware of Human living almost by instinct or autopilot, reacting to situations where you feel as if you are being victimised. Here your life can feel out of control, but it is not. Your life is always under control because what is happening in the now is meant to happen. There is no right or wrong in your life's journey. Even the mistakes you make are there to guide you. Whether you allow life to teach you is your choice. If you don't, it will take longer for you to find life and the abundance of it, but this is still not wrong. Yes, you may feel that because of your choices, you have caused yourself and others unnecessary hardship, but that in itself may also have purpose. I realise that more questions than answers are raised when trying to understand life. We see so much hardship and pain which seems wrong, but don't try to understand it. Instead, accept it and do your best to bring peace and love to the world, starting in your inner circle, where there is no more hurting of other people because you choose for Divine to rule.

Be aware of the support of the whole universe behind you. Notice the smile of the stranger passing by. What did the person see in you to make them smile? Just when you need some encouragement, you will notice friends that you have not heard from in months phoning you unexpectedly to see how you are. You will notice that somehow there is enough money even when you thought all was lost. You will become aware that there is something or someone far bigger than you can imagine who cares. That someone is love, which cares and has always been with you but needs to have contact with your Divine as your true self. The blockages will start falling away through a renewal of your mind where Divine rules.

All will be well as you build on your relationship with your Creator. This is only the beginning; your teacher will appear when you are ready. You are more than able to find your own way through a relationship with your Creator. I urge you to explore Jesus, or Yeshua the messiah, with your Divine because there is something about this man that changed the lives of those who were with him. I don't want you to think that this book is pushing some doctrine, but this man made a way, I believe, for you and me to connect with our Creator. You must embark on your own journey of discovery; and through Sam, you will make your own discoveries, as Sam has a way of teaching you, of making you notice those seemingly small happenings that can change your world as your mind becomes a different place.

I wish you well and hope that you may experience a renewal of your mind as you enter this place of awareness. Know that you are not alone—that those who are closest to you want only the best for you, although Human will say otherwise. Find Divine, find your Creator, and find life.

Expect to wake up in the morning knowing that it's another day of miracles, because you are health, you are love, you are success. The truth in who you are as Divine will escalate each day to a place where you realise that nothing is impossible. You will find a life that matters through a connection with your Creator, knowing that you, God, and the world around you are all one. If we could all get to this place, there would be no murders, no rapes, and no sickness, but make it your responsibility to change your space. Human does not like the word accountability so practice this by being accountable for your well-being.

Thoughts of hopelessness are a lie created by Human. Divine is standing by waiting for you to make the choice to be childlike in your dependency and trust in your Creator, who is there for you, who wants you to experience the love that is yours. As previously mentioned, sons and daughters do not have to do anything to earn the love from their parents; they are born into that love. The same applies to you and me. Our Creator made us, birthed us as spirit beings into this universe, and did everything to enable you and me to have that spirit-to-spirit connection which brings our lives to a place of peace as we grasp the reality of our Creator's love for us all. It's a place where sleep does not become a form of escape but rather where waking up is a joy. Take time out to go and shout out aloud where no one can hear you; do something different. Find that willingness in you to love and be grateful for everything, even your darkest hour. Human can't rule when you are in this place, and it's time for your Divine to change everything.

I want you to try this tool that has helped me. I encourage you to write at least a two-page letter to Yahweh, or God, or whoever you see as your Lord, at least twice a week, every day if you like. Simply write without stopping. Write about how you are feeling and what your needs are. Write as if you were speaking to Yahweh, who you know loves you dearly and simply wants you to talk. Have the faith at that moment to say thank you with conviction. Be aware as best as you can of allowing Divine, that part of you that has a direct contact with your Creator, to do the writing.

My own journey has been one where I have always had enough. The home I was raised in always had enough. I had wonderful parents who did their best in raising me, for which I will always be grateful. As I have grown older, I have questioned the reasons for not being able to experience more than 'just enough'—and guess who the culprit was. The one and only Human. My Divine was there, but Divine was unable to manifest my dreams, because of the blockages caused by Human. How did I remove those blockages? An awareness of a childlike mindset, where there was a giving over to my Creator through my Divine, rather than operating through my Human mindset which had set limitations which I was not even aware of. That childlikeness forms a dependency on something bigger within you, giving you peace in every situation.

The reality is that you have come from a source that has no limit, and therefore you have no limitations as a spirit being. I can assure you that your life will change through a renewed awareness of the role that Human plays in your life. Use this to rid yourself of the blockages which emanate from Human, allowing Divine to rule your mind and consequently your soul.

There may well be days or periods of time where doubt will be your partner and loneliness will consume you, but please remember that Divine will never leave you. It will take determination from your part to counteract these negative emotions by giving yourself time to meditate. Read affirmations that are important to you; read extracts of books that have spoken to you. Be aware of your thoughts and choose to keep them true to Divine rather than allowing Human to plant seeds of doubt, anger, and pity, which only occur because Human does not want you to grasp how big you are as Divine. Complete acceptance of who you are is required, knowing that this is a daily walk and that none of us have arrived, rest in the fact that this is a lifelong journey full of wonder as you discover your original greatness that you lost along the way.

Your talents will become evident, and your dreams will become clearer. You will find your purpose. You will find that your life matters. An element of serving becomes all-important as Divine takes over as your newfound self.

I would encourage you to spend time in being 'still' in a way that works best for you; for when the mind is calmed and you are in a place of peace, there is a growth of spirit. With Divine at the helm, all will be good. You will build a relationship with your Maker, this God of love, a God who has plans for you and me—plans for you to prosper, be a blessing to those around you, and bring comfort to those who feel that their situations are hopeless. There is no judgement for those in this place; be grateful when you are not in this place.

Allow your awareness to guide you to a place of stillness, that place in you where unconditional love is found. You can retreat to this place whenever you choose. Don't try to justify that you can't; the choice is yours. Learn to shift your energy, thereby finding that place where no offence can take place. You are the creator of your world and can change everything by operating from that place of stillness, which is love itself. You need to become acutely aware of every word you speak, every thought you think. Whenever you use the word "I" take note in that this is more than likely a Human moment. If the words you are about to speak are not based on kindness or gratitude, precondition yourself to be quiet, as this will limit the destructive role of Human. Every word needs to be uplifting. There is no justification in anything less than this. There will be times when others may take offence to what you say, but this is only their Humans that they struggle with, making them no different to you or me. Be prepared to say sorry if required too. Remember that you don't have to be wrong to apologise. Say you're sorry because of the possibility of hurting the other person in some way, even if it is his or her own Human that is causing this hurt. Be aware of your energy. Is it coming from a place of love or judgement, from Divine or Human?

As you choose more of Divine, you will find that what would have led you previously into battle is now in a way detached from you, enabling you to grasp the bigger picture of understanding the futility of strife. Be sure to treat those close to you with mercy and compassion. Something in you may want to bring strife into a time of peace. Be aware of this because Human is saying that you don't deserve the peace; therefore, you subconsciously sabotage that very peace that is rightfully yours.

Surrender the need to control and to understand everything; recognise that this is Human. Be aware that Human will always undermine every attempt to create harmony and intimacy. Human wants to win because with Human there has to be a loser; otherwise, nothing has been gained. From the time we are small, our minds are conditioned this way. We partake in races and competitions and strive to win. When we lose, we feel bad, so the next time we try to feel better by winning at all costs, and in the process, someone else feels as though he has not measured up. And so the madness continues.

Remember that Human has a way of being its own worst enemy. Even when you recognise that you are causing pain to yourself and others, there is this attitude of not really caring, this mindset of "If I am feeling unimportant or hurt, then you can also suffer." No matter how far removed this mindset may be from Divine, you will still find yourself choosing this destructive path. Don't condemn yourself when this happens; choose to let go of it instead. Don't fight it, for this is not the real you, and saying sorry will release the negative energy. Remember that Human will justify not saying sorry. The choice is yours.

As you become aware of the needs of others around you and how your thoughts and emotions impact them, your own day-to-day concerns become less of an issue. The beauty of this is that your day-to-day concerns will resolve themselves with little effort from you.

Having peace and joy is something that we all strive for. The truth is that you are that peace, you are that joy, and you are that abundance. It is in you; it is part of you. Not believing this is like a qualified physician asking to be re-enrolled in a university for a second time to study to be a doctor again because he doesn't believe that he is a doctor. This would be a never-ending process which denies the truth that he or she is a doctor capable of helping the sick. I know this sound ridiculous, but this is what is happening when we don't want to accept who we are as Divine.

You may be in such a sad place that you feel that trying is of no use because you simply cannot even imagine yourself being of any worth. Listen to me when I say that this is a lie that you cannot afford to entertain. I know you are wonderfully made; I have no doubt about that. You have qualities in you that are like diamonds, like precious stones. Just maybe the very Maker of the universe is on your side, just maybe you will feel that love saturating your very being, that there will be a knowing that you are not alone, that all will be good because you are good. Remember here that Divine says yes and Human says no, which are you going to choose?

Usually it is only when we are in that sad place, that sick place, that lonely place, that tired place that we say we've had enough of the lies that life has taught us. Allow Sam to teach you through the awareness of your choices. This is a different experience for each one of us, but I ask you to allow it to take place. Trust in the love that is within you. Reach out to the source of your Creator and don't try to understand God, for again Human can trap you. Remember that 'childlikeness' deletes the concept of having to understand everything, be at peace about this; this principle is life changing, and we need to follow this through in our thought patterns. It is never too late for change, whether you are twelve years old or ninety years old. After all, you are eternal. Go out there and change everything. You have the resources within you. You are magnificent and wonderful in every way, a creator. Go and create who you want to be.

In your renewed awareness, Human will be exposed because when the truth is made known, Human has nothing to hang on to and automatically loses grip. You will experience your true self.

We spoke about the kingdom of God, and that this is a turnaround in the conventional way you think. This can only come about through a spirit-to-spirit communication with your Creator as you become aware of your true identity as Divine. As mentioned previously, you will experience a resistance to this mind shift, and I urge you to push forward and not be discouraged by any possible subconscious efforts to sabotage the very life and abundance that is yours.

The universe is behind you cheering you on. Opportunities will unfold before you that were always there but were blocked by a mind ruled by Human. You may well have wanted to do something but felt that you did not have whatever was needed to do it. Be aware that this could be Human sabotaging what you are meant to do. Remember that within you is the I AM that has no fear, that cannot be offended. Lift up your hands and rejoice because you are wonderful, powerful, beautiful, and precious. Know that because it is the truth.

Remember to be aware of what mindset you are operating from, Human or Divine. The awareness must become part of you, allowing you to make the choice moment by moment.

Your world will change as your Divine shows you the way. You are far greater than you can even imagine. Discover the life that you were created to live. Now is the time to unlock your true self. Embody Divine and receive the truth in who you are, which will go beyond your present reality. I wish you a wonderful life filled with joy as you discover that wonderful limitlessness within you because of the source from which you were made and which is part of you. That source created the universe, and you cannot get much bigger than that.

I trust that this book will bring about that awareness of who you are not. I hope I have brought you a measure of comfort in the knowledge of your true self. Expect miracles and don't allow the past wrong beliefs to block the miracles, for Divine is the miracle worker and needs to rule your heart.

Learn how to manage Human through Sam so that Divine can rule. Through Sam, make a choice to be aware of the love in you, your Divine, showing compassion, mercy, and kindness, with no judgement.

Let's summarise the fundamentals of obtaining the change in mindset required for Divine to rule in your mind, heart, and soul.

Childlikeness

See yourself as a small child being tossed into the air and caught as maybe your father did with you. Feel the delight of the sensation of floating in the air for that brief moment, knowing that you would fall but that Dad was there to catch you. There was no doubt of that, so you enjoyed the moment. It's the same for you and me. We may feel at times that we are living on the edge as it were, but maybe it is just Yahweh that is throwing us in the air, so enjoy the moment rather than allowing fear to take over. You will be caught and thrown up again so enjoy the ride.

Awareness of Human and Divine

I think you will agree that the importance of this component has been made clear. Without an awareness of Divine or Human, there is no choice, and as Human is our default side, operating as our false self, we will then experience more of the same.

Meditation

This is covered in chapter 11. Note that without some form of meditation to bring you to that still place, change will be difficult.

Your Creator sees you as you were made

Let's remind ourselves that our Creator sees us as the spirit beings made in the image of love. What you have done or not done is not the issue; it's who you are that needs to become your reality.

Receive what is yours

We are raised with the concept that we have to earn whatever we receive. Well, this is not the case concerning the kingdom of God's principles, in that we cannot earn our Creator's love. It is unconditional love and needs to be received as such by Divine. Human cannot receive this love, for with Human, it has to be earned.

Need no protection

Remember that you are in a safe place because your Divine is found in the Kingdom of God, which is a safe place, and therefore protection is not an issue. However, with Human it is an issue because it does not recognise the Kingdom of God, or the safety of this place.

Not alone

Remember that the universe (God) is behind you and will guide you through the day by drawing your attention to different things, from something you read to seeing someone who reminds you of someone else you may need to contact. Know that nothing is coincidental. Be aware that Human wants to convince you otherwise.

Surrender Human

Don't fight Human because you will then only experience more of the same. Human has a role as your intellect, but it must not be your master.

You are love

Life tells us that we are not lovely or magnificent because of what we have experienced, mainly in our early years. This could have been your father making you feel that you didn't measure up in some way, that perhaps he did not say he loved you as much as he ought to have.

Know that you are magnificent. You are made in the image of your Maker, who is love, and as such, you too are love. Don't allow Human to convince you otherwise. It's time for your Divine to stand up.

Treat others as you would have them treat you

Divine lives by the principle of treating others as you would have them treat you. Human says that if people behave like idiots, they should expect to be treated as such.

Divine does not focus on the idiots but rather the Divine in the idiots and will treat them all as they would want to be treated.

Let's end by reminding ourselves that to find our true selves, there needs to be an awareness of Human and the destructive energy that is created from this mindset. Sam will guide us in our moment-by-moment choices in words and thoughts. Are our thoughts coming from a place of unconditional love with no judgement, or are we trying to justify our own misery by creating discord and further misery around us through the judgement of others and ourselves?

Divine is in all people that cross your path, where their spoken words may well speak to the core of your soul; written words that are meant for you will become alive to you. Remember that money is your friend, health is your ally, and all has been accomplished for you to receive life and the fullness of it. Remember you have no end just as the universe has no end, you are one with the universe and with your Creator. Divine must rule as your mindest, now and for eternity not Human and we know that a mindset dominated by Human only brings fear and uncertainty.

It is time for your true self to reign every moment of every day through your own free-will choice. You came into this world as that magnificent being of love and as such cannot remain hidden behind a false identity created by a Human mindset. It is time for your Divine to rule as love, creating your own wonderful life. My heart's desire is for you to know your Creator and to experience a life of love emanating from you and towards you.

Broken hearts are restored through Divine. Divine will set you free from whatever may be holding you captive in Human. Human may want you to put this book down and forget what you have read as quickly as possible. If this is the case, be aware of this. I know I keep repeating this aspect of Human's interference, but Human is so subtle that often it is like a snare that one walks into because you don't remember to be aware of who is ruling at any given moment and you experience only more of the same.

Experience the peace and joy that is yours. This is not earned; it is yours. You were born with this peace and joy, with a connection to your Creator, but this is lost along the way because of the Human in those closest to you and in the world that causes you to believe that you are someone you are not. Take hold of your Divine as your true identity, and as you do this, your love will ignite the Divine in others.

I would encourage you to highlight sentences in this book that have spoken to you so that you can read them over and over as they will cancel out the lies and fears that you may struggle to rid yourself of. You do need to try and find a support base as it were in a friend or group of friends, as this process of finding Divine is not a solo one. I encourage you to visit my website (www.whorulesyourmind.com.), where I will provide material that will encourage you, as your Human will not take this change lying down.

Your Creator sees you as the wonderful Divine being you are and its time that you see yourself as your Creator sees you because in this place you allow your Creator to change your world.

About the Author

Mark is a professional technologist in engineering with a heart for people. His passion is to help those who desire to break free from the struggles of life that might at times want to consume them. Mark creates an awareness of the power of love within each one of us and the changes this brings to our own lives and those closest to us.

Website: www.whorulesyourmind.com

About the Book

Who Rules Your Mind?

T his book will bring an awareness of a false side of you that will sabotage almost everything that was intended to bring peace and joy to your life. This false side of you creates an identity in the absence of you not knowing your true identity as a spirit being where love abounds, where there is no judgement of others or yourself.

The realisation of your true self as the spirit being of love that you are and its oneness with the universe and its Creator will bring about the mindshift that is needed to make the necessary choices to change your thoughts around your identity, thereby enabling you to change your life. The toiling will cease as you learn to give over to your true self, that which is childlike in nature and rests in the knowledge that you are never alone.